# Raising
# Healthy Eaters

# Raising Healthy Eaters

## 100 Tips for Parents

### Henry Legere, M.D.

Da Capo
LIFE
LONG

A Member of the Perseus Book Group

Copyright © 2004 by Henry Joseph Legere III
Food Guide Pyramid for Young Children © the U.S. Department of Agriculture. Used by permission.

Set in 9.25-point Stone Serif by The Perseus Books Group

Cataloging-in-Publication data for this book is available from the Library of Congress.

First printing 2004
ISBN 0–7382–0963–5
Scholastic Edition 0–7382–1047–1

Published by Da Capo Press
A Member of the Perseus Books Group
http://www.dacapopress.com

Da Capo Press books are available at special discounts for bulk purchases in the U.S. by corporations, institutions, and other organizations. For more information, please contact the Special Markets Department at the Perseus Books Group, 11 Cambridge Center, Cambridge, MA 02142, or call (800) 255–1514 or (617) 252–5298, or email special.markets@perseusbooks.com.

1 2 3 4 5 6 7 8 9—08 07 06 05

*For Claudia and Chloe with love*

# Contents

# Introduction

There is an overwhelming amount of information available to parents today concerning everything to do with being a parent. As a pediatrician and advocate for families, I try in every patient encounter to clarify the confusing messages coming from various sources. Of foremost concern to parents during well-child visits is how to raise a healthy eater in a fast-food culture.

Obesity has reached epidemic proportions among our children. Both the American Academy of Pediatricians and the Academy of Family Practitioners have declared as much. The American Medical Association predicts that the increased costs of medical problems resulting from obesity will cost society billions of dollars in the years to come. In addition to the morbidity associated with obesity, the consequences of poor dietary habits include increased risk of heart disease, stroke, diabetes, vision loss, renal disease, and certain types of cancer.

Given this information, you might be tempted to put your chubby little baby on a diet. However, as a general rule, children should not diet! Some dieting, when implemented by a pediatrician, may be safe and even warranted. However, children who begin deprivation diets start the vicious cycle of yo-yoing that can affect their metabolism, their growth, and their endocrine system. The best way to maintain a healthy weight is to maintain a healthy eating regimen from the start. Children who are fit will stay fit. Children who are not fit can engage in the process of becoming fit, adopting patterns of eating and behavior that will increase their lean body mass, their metabolism, their energy level, and their confidence and self-esteem. Healthy eating is a lifestyle, not a fad. As such, it is a process that needs to be learned over years and reinforced by consistent rules and by parents who are good role models.

As a pediatrician, I've had the opportunity to listen to parents' complaints about some of the common obstacles to raising a healthy eater. Furthermore, I have the benefit of mentors who have listened to parents' complaints for some twenty to thirty years longer than I have and who have seen what works and what doesn't. This book is the by-product of all that combined experience. The 100 tips provided here can serve as your guide to initiating the process of raising a healthy eater.

To make this book as user-friendly as possible, I have organized the 100 tips into six chapters: "Understanding Nutrition," "The Basic Rules of Raising a Healthy Eater," "Troubleshooting for Picky Eaters," "Meals, Snacks, and Beverages," "Activity," and finally, "Nutrition and Health Issues."

Several of the tips provide general dietary lessons that clarify and demystify what it means to eat healthy. Each tip contains an explanation filled with high-yield, easy-to-understand-and-utilize information. One tip provides information on the correct interpretation of the food pyramid and elucidates the role of each meal and the major nutrients. Other tips incorporate this knowledge into meal planning and give additional ideas on attaining the enthusiastic cooperation of our future healthy eaters.

Many of the tips are geared to overcoming the common obstacles of healthy eating for specific age groups of children, such as fussy eaters and milk-o-holics.

Some of the tips are addressed to families who are vegetarian or "whole-foods" consumers, providing healthy recipes and fun activities. In this vein, there are also tips for recognizing the benefits and pitfalls of organic foods. Additionally, I have included several tips for building self-esteem and a healthy body image as part of a healthy dietary regimen as it relates to preventing the eating disorders and medical diseases that can result from unhealthy eating habits.

There is no magic pill, no panacea, that will cure a society's poor eating habits. Parents can do only so much to protect their children. As children get older they become more responsible for their own choices. Unfortunately, some of the choices they make can affect their future health. Each family must make their own choices, and parents must do their utmost to give their children every opportunity to be healthy in the years to come. These tips are geared toward establishing a sustainable dietary regimen that will give children a head start in the lifelong process of healthy eating. Good luck and have fun!

# CHAPTER 1

# Understanding Nutrition

*Nutrition is what we put in our mouths and the mouths of our children. Everything you and your child eat can be broken down into a few groups: things you get energy from, things your body uses to form tissues and bones, things that promote bowel movements, things your body uses to facilitate chemical reactions at the molecular level, and finally, things that can affect your body in other ways, either positively or negatively, like medications or caffeine.*

*At the simplest level, eating a well-balanced diet with foods from each of the major food groups ensures that you and your children are eating healthy without ever having to think about it. To help keep nutrition simple, here are some tips that address different categories of nutrients.*

## Tip 1
## Carbohydrates should be the foundation of your children's healthy diets.

Despite the popularity of recent high-protein diets that vilify dietary carbohydrates, carbohydrates are the foundation of a sustainable, healthy diet for you and your kids. Although it is true that excessive carbohydrates are converted to fat, the same can be said of dietary protein and fat. High-protein diets work in the short run because dieters are taking in fewer calories than they are burning. The high-protein foods that are the staple of fad diets are often high in fat, and the long-term effects of high cholesterol on dieters' cardiac health are still unknown. Furthermore, much of the weight loss credited to a high-protein diet over the short run is lost water weight. Walking around partially dehydrated is not good for anyone, especially children!

When I give advice to my patients and their parents, I ask myself what I would tell my brothers and sisters about feeding my nephews and nieces, and I think about what I recommend for my own daughter. In sum, I never recommend fad diets to my own family. Small children should certainly not be on nutrient-restrictive diets unless they are followed closely by a pediatrician and dietitian. Teens too should not start dabbling with fad diets, which can begin the lifelong process of yo-yoing—repeated weight loss and weight gain—that plagues so many. Like so many things in life, carbohydrates are good in moderation. That said, whole-wheat bread, brown rice, and wheat pasta are better choices than their white or processed counterparts for the whole family.

## Tip 2
## Incorporate nonmeat sources of protein into your child's diet.

Giving your child a combination of protein sources is the optimal way to raise a healthy eater. Your children need to consume 10% to 15% of their daily calories from protein sources to ensure adequate growth and tissue repair, but the typical child's diet provides twice the amount of protein needed. Regardless if your child eats too many calories from protein, carbohydrate, or fat, extra calories are stored as fat by his body. The key to healthy eating is understanding that protein is available from sources other than meat, which, in addition to being high in protein, is often high in fat.

So what's the difference between animal-derived protein and plant-derived protein? Both are made up of the same set of twenty amino acids. Animal-derived proteins are called complete because they contain all of the needed amino acids in each bite. Plant-derived proteins are incomplete because they do not. However, by combining plant protein sources, such as rice and beans, you are providing your child with all of the needed amino acids!

As parents struggle to lower cholesterol and improve their families' cardiovascular health, they are faced with the challenge of meeting their children's protein needs while at the same time reducing saturated fat and cholesterol in their diets. Natural and convenient alternatives are readily available in the form of beans and soy protein. The American Heart Association has proclaimed that dietary soy protein can lower LDL, or so-called "bad" cholesterol. Not only are beans affordable and great sources of protein, but they also contain needed B vitamins, iron, and calcium. Furthermore, they are rich in fiber and cholesterol-free.

Feed your kids a healthy, well-rounded diet centered on the principles of variety and moderation and obtain the benefits from both meat and nonmeat sources of proteins.

## Tip 3
## Not all fat is bad.

So what's the skinny on fat? Many misconceptions about fat are perpetuated by fad-dieting, as well as a frenzy of information about the risks and benefits of high-fat diets. What is clear is that a prudent diet for children includes moderate consumption of saturated fat and cholesterol. Indeed, an adequate amount of fat is necessary since fats and cholesterol serve not only as a source of energy but as important building blocks for cells and hormones. Healthy eating patterns with moderate fat consumption in childhood are linked to a reduction in heart disease, diabetes, and obesity in adulthood. So an ounce of prevention is worth a pound of cure!

All that being said, it's important to remember that not all fats are equal. Saturated fats are the worst kind. Choose cooking oils that contain polyunsaturated and monounsaturated fats, like olive oil. A good rule of thumb is that unsaturated fats are liquids at room temperature and are generally derived from plants, while saturated fats are solids at room temperature and are typically derived from animals.

When shopping for snacks for your kids, you should also avoid partially hydrogenated fats, like those found in many store-bought cookies, crackers, and baked goods. Keep in mind that soft margarine is generally better for you and your children than stick margarine because it has fewer trans-fatty acids. Trans-fatty acids are associated with an increased risk of heart disease because they lead to an increase in the bad type of cholesterol.

## Tip 4
## Teach your children the new food pyramid guidelines and incorporate these guidelines into your dietary planning.

As complicated as the new food pyramid might seem (see appendix A or visit www.usda.gov), adhering to the guidelines is not rocket science. With a little planning and a smidgen of self-discipline, you can teach your children a systematic approach to eating healthy that will last their whole lives. The food pyramid guidelines for older children and adults are slightly different from the guidelines for young children between the ages of two and six, for whom the U.S. Department of Agriculture created modified recommendations endorsed by the American Academy of Pediatricians:

- Six daily servings from the grain and cereal group

- Three daily servings of vegetables

- Two daily servings from the fruit group

- Two daily servings of meat and two of milk and dairy

The main difference between these recommendations for little kids and those for the rest of the family is that the quantity of the servings is different for big people and little people. For everyone, variety is key.

Here's a helpful tip I got from a colleague. She calls it the Five-Plus Rule. She recommends that families strive to eat a minimum of five servings of fruit and vegetables, but you don't have to stop there. Up to ten servings a day is okay.

Another great new way of thinking about the food pyramid that is gaining steam among pediatricians is to teach younger children about "everyday" foods and "sometime" foods. Everyday foods are the healthy foods that fill in the base of the food pyramid and should be eaten daily. Sometime foods, like ice cream, cookies, cake, and candy, are at the very top and should be eaten sparingly—during holidays, for instance, or as a once-a-week treat. Once your kids understand the distinction, they'll probably start to tell *you* which is which and take responsibility for their own treats.

## Tip 5
## A well-balanced diet is an adequate source of water-soluble vitamins.

For the whole of human history, most people have obtained all the vitamins and minerals they needed without ever taking a Flintstones vitamin. Don't get me wrong, I take my Flintstones equivalent every day for good measure, but if you follow the food pyramid guidelines, your children *should* be able to get all of the vitamins and minerals they need from their diets.

Here is a helpful list of important water-soluble vitamins and the dietary sources from which they are derived.

**Thiamin, or vitamin B$_1$:** Needed for normal functioning of muscle tissues, including the heart, the nervous system, and the digestive system, B$_1$ also serves an important role in carbohydrate metabolism and energy production. Lean meats, nuts and beans, and enriched and fortified cereals are great sources of vitamin B$_1$.

**Riboflavin, or vitamin B$_2$:** Needed for energy production, normal immune function, and healthy skin, B$_2$ is easily obtained from foods like lean meat, eggs, cereals, green leafy vegetables, and dairy products.

**Niacin, or vitamin B$_3$:** Comes from foods such as lean meats, nuts and beans, cereals, and yeasts and is needed for energy production, for maintaining normal skin, and as a digestive aid. It can be made by your body from the dietary intake of the amino acid tryptophan.

**Folic acid:** Needed for energy production, preventing anemia, and preventing birth defects such as neural tube defects, folic acid can be easily obtained from meats, beans, leafy greens, and whole grains.

**Vitamin B$_{12}$, or cobalamin:** This vitamin comes only from animal-derived products, such as meat and dairy. B$_{12}$ is important for energy production, anemia prevention, utilization of folic acid, and nervous system function.

**Biotin:** Needed for many of the intracellular reactions that lead to energy production, biotin is so widespread in the foods your kids eat that deficiencies of this nutrient are unheard of in developed countries.

**Vitamin C, or ascorbic acid:** Found in citrus fruits, berries, tomatoes, potatoes, and leafy green vegetables, among other foods, vitamin C is needed for normal growth, immune function, wound healing, bone and tooth formation, and efficient iron absorption.

As you can see, if your children are eating well-balanced diets that include foods from all of the food groups, they will get all of the water-soluble vitamins they need without the help of Fred or Barney. Refer to tip 14 for a more specific discussion of whether your child should take a daily multivitamin.

## Tip 6
## Encourage your kids to eat a diet rich in fiber.

Planting the seed for good health maintenance begins with fiber. My doctor once told me that fiber is like a broom for the GI tract, sweeping its way through the intestines. Sources of fiber are abundant, including fresh fruits, vegetables, whole grains, legumes, and seeds. A typical American diet contains only five to ten grams of dietary fiber a day, much lower than the recommended twenty to thirty-five grams a day. High-fiber diets reduce constipation, straining with bowel movements, rectal fissures, hemorrhoids, and diverticular disease as your kids become older adults. Furthermore, high-fiber diets may help to reduce the incidence of certain gastrointestinal cancers.

Many snack foods are made from refined flour and sugar, so just remember to include some snacks that have fiber in them when planning your kid's menu. For example, one apple has about three grams of fiber, one slice of whole-wheat bread has two grams of fiber, and one carrot has two grams of fiber. If one food doesn't appeal, try another. If you can't get your little ones to eat bran baked goods, peel an orange for them. Air-popped popcorn as a snack is also a good source of fiber, or get your kids to eat a salad with their meals.

Some kids may have bloating, cramping, and increased gas as the amount of fiber in their diet is increased. For this reason, it is important to encourage your child to drink a lot of liquid when adding fiber to her diet and to make these changes gradually over time.

## Tip 7
## Ensure that your growing kids are getting enough calcium.

During periods of growth, children, and especially teenagers, need additional nutrients. This means your growing kids require more calories and more essential vitamins and minerals. One of the most important minerals that your children need more of during periods of rapid growth is calcium. However, according to the USDA, fewer than 35% of boys and fewer than 15% of girls take in the recommended daily allowance (RDA) of calcium.

Taking in and utilizing enough calcium helps your children attain maximal bone densities, which is one of the best defenses against developing osteoporosis later in life. Calcium is also an important intracellular molecule that is responsible for muscle contraction and chemical signaling.

Because close to half of your children's bone mass is developed during adolescence, teenagers need about 25% to 40% more calcium in their diets than do people of other ages. This translates into between 1,200 and 1,500 milligrams of calcium a day! Though that sounds like a lot, keep in mind that a cup of yogurt has almost 200 milligrams of calcium, or 15% of what your adolescent needs in a day, and a glass of milk has over 400 milligrams, or 30%.

## Tip 8
## Stock the refrigerator with healthy, caffeine-free beverages.

Should you be uneasy over how much caffeine your child consumes? It depends. Used judiciously, caffeine improves concentration because it acts as a mild stimulant to the central nervous system. However, even moderate consumption can lead to undesirable side effects such as nervousness, irritability, sleeplessness, and rapid heart rate. Caffeine also leads to increased urination because it is a diuretic. This can cause problems with bedwetting in younger children, and it can also lead to problems with dehydration in children who are active and using caffeine-containing beverages to rehydrate.

Foods and beverages with high amounts of caffeine, such as coffee, cola, tea, chocolate, and over-the-counter medications, can also make it more difficult for your child to fall asleep. Caffeine-associated headaches and fatigue secondary to sleeplessness may lead to poor school performance.

Given all this, keep caffeine in mind when shopping and keep it out of the refrigerator. Opt instead to stock up on healthy caffeine-free beverages like skim and low-fat milk, fruit juice, and especially water. Also, encourage older children to choose caffeine-free alternatives like decaf espresso drinks and herbal teas when visiting cafés with friends.

## Tip 9
## Beware of hidden sugars in your children's foods.

Your kids are probably eating quite a bit more sugar than you realize. The average American consumed about 125 pounds of added sugar in 1980, 160 pounds in 1999, and 165 pounds in 2002! Food producers have become much more sophisticated when it comes to hiding more sugar in your kids' foods. Even if you don't think of your family as having a sweet tooth, they are taking in hidden sugars in everything from ketchup to healthy foods such as yogurt.

Why are companies doing this? First of all, food producers sneak in some insulin-spiking hidden sugars in an attempt to increase the flavor in foods that have been reduced in salt and fat. Secondly, and more obviously, they know that kids love to eat sweet things.

Some nutritionists separate sugars into two categories: the high-glycemic-response sugars and the low-glycemic-response sugars. It is the high-glycemic sugars that you should moderate. These include sucrose, glucose, dextrose, evaporated cane juice, maltodextrin, galactose, corn syrup, dextrin, beet sugar, raw sugar, brown sugar, white sugar, concentrated fruit juice, syrup, sorghum, honey, maple syrup, and high-fructose corn syrup. Foods like ketchup, jams, jellies, soft drinks, fruit juice, canned fruit, ice cream, pastries, and candies can also be packed with starches that turn into high-glycemic sugars.

Obviously, it's going to be hard to cut out high-glycemic sugars altogether, but there are a couple of easy steps you can take to dramatically reduce your child's sugar intake:

- Limit the sugary cereals your kids eat. Instead, use fruit to sweeten your kids' cereal.

- Encourage your kids to get their nutrients and energy from whole foods like fruit and nuts, not from energy bars and sugary drinks.

- Finally, when buying fruit juice, stay away from those labeled "from concentrate" and buy "100% fruit juice" instead, then dilute it with water. Don't be tricked by drinks that have terms like "100% natural" or some similar slogan that is 100% nonsense.

## Tip 10
## Serve at least three servings
## a day of whole-grained foods.

A whole grain is any grain that still has all three parts of its grain kernel intact: the bran, germ, and endosperm. Grains are no longer whole or as wholesome when they are refined, since they lose the fiber-rich bran and the nutrient-rich germ.

According to the Food and Drug Administration (FDA), only about 5% of Americans eat three servings of whole grains a day. The major health benefit of whole grains is their ability to protect against chronic diseases. The FDA has announced that foods made with at least 51% whole grains act as potential heart disease and cancer fighters. More specifically, eating a diet rich in whole grains can decrease your child's risk for cardiovascular disease, colon cancer, and obesity. Whole grains contain high levels of fiber, vitamins, and minerals. The health benefits of whole grains come from a combination of all of these substances and cannot be replaced by the enrichment process.

Here are some helpful tips for choosing whole-grained foods:

- The first ingredient listed on a label for whole-grained bread should be whole-wheat flour, not enriched wheat flour.

- Choose nutrient quality and taste over convenience. Generally speaking, foods that require more cooking time (basmati rice or whole oats oatmeal) have whole grains compared to their non-whole-grained counterfeits (minute rice or instant oatmeal). The few extra minutes of preparation will be worth the wait in flavor, texture, and nutrients.

- Don't trust the color when choosing whole-grained food products. Brown does not always mean healthy. Bread can be darkened with additives such as molasses to give it the appearance of whole-grained bread.

## Tip 11
## Make sure your kids have an iron-rich diet.

It is hard to believe that mineral deficiencies exist in a developed country, but believe it or not, iron deficiency is still all too common in our society. According to the Centers for Disease Control (CDC), iron deficiency exists in the United States to a degree sufficient to have an impact on intellectual growth in as many as one in fourteen toddlers and one in six teenage girls. This means that millions of children are affected! Toddlers, prekindergarten children, and menstruating teenage girls are three high-risk age groups that need to be ensured an iron-rich diet.

Children and parents might not notice the symptoms of iron deficiency, which can include decreased memory, poor school performance, impaired athletic performance, fatigue, irritability, headaches, and poor appetite. Kids with iron deficiency anemia tend to get sick more often. Children can usually get all the iron they need from a healthy diet; nonetheless, they should be screened at the appropriate ages during visits to the pediatrician to determine if they are getting enough iron.

The foods highest in iron are lean, red meats, raisins, spinach, and nuts, but iron can be found in varying amounts in almost all green vegetables as well as in nonred meats such as fish and poultry. Some children may need iron supplementation in addition to an iron-rich diet. Talk to your pediatrician about your child's individual iron needs.

## Tip 12
## Offer only water or sugar-free beverages with meals.

For kids older than two and a half to three years old, parents need to institute an early routine of offering only water, non-fat milk, or sugar-free beverages with meals. Three-year-olds should be drinking from cups, and yet I often see them walk into my clinic with a security bottle filled with juice or soda. Judging by their plumpness and poor dental health, I can tell they probably don't go anywhere without their companion bottle permanently attached to their lips. In addition to promoting tooth decay, these ever-present bottles of juice or soda are simply not providing much nutritional value.

Sure, kids need water, so give them water, nonfat milk, or at worst sugar-free, noncarbonated beverages. For the most part, soda and juices are merely sugar water. I'm the last person to say that flavor doesn't matter, and for most of my life I wouldn't touch any liquid that wasn't flavored. Flavored doesn't have to mean sweetened, though, and sweetened doesn't have to mean sugared. There are numerous options available to parents. Squeeze some lemon juice into water to add flavor, or offer sugar-free Kool-Aid as an alternative to soda. For juice-a-holics, dilute cranberry juice with water as a reduced-calorie alternative. You can gradually decrease the amount of juice in the mixture until your kids become used to drinking unsweetened beverages.

## Tip 13
## Combine fatty foods with green vegetables for better vitamin absorption.

Fatty acids come from the consumption of dietary fat and are vital for your child's health. Fatty acids are important sources of energy for the heart, building blocks for cell membranes, and essential elements in normal neurologic development.

Additionally, dietary fat is necessary to absorb fat-soluble vitamins, including vitamins A, D, E, and K. Vitamin A supports night vision and keeps skin healthy. Vitamin D helps the body absorb and use calcium, which is essential for healthy bones. Vitamin E keeps red blood cells healthy and may prevent cancer through its antioxidant effects. Vitamin K is necessary for the normal clotting of blood and may play a role in skeletal health.

Your child should be getting these vitamins from his daily diet, since fat-soluble vitamins are stored in the body and it is possible to achieve toxic levels of vitamins A and D if you give your child excessive supplements. Excessive supplementation is not always easy to quantify because each child clears differing amounts of fat-soluble vitamins from his system. In general, you should not give your children supplements that give more than 200% of the recommended daily allowance of individual nutrients. If you offer your child green, leafy vegetables instead of a vitamin supplement, this won't be an issue.

Try this healthy vegetable dish. Cut up asparagus, yellow, red, and green bell peppers, and shallots and place them all on a cookie sheet. Sprinkle olive oil and a little salt over the vegetables. Bake the vegetables in the oven for ten to twenty minutes, or until done. The combined colors, textures, and flavors of this vegetable medley will be enticing to your children to eat and will simultaneously maximize the absorption of the fat-soluble vitamins contained in them.

## Tip 14
## Children need vitamins and minerals every day, but not necessarily a daily multivitamin.

Do children need to take vitamins? Yes! And no! Vitamins and minerals are vital for normal growth and development, but children who eat well-balanced diets usually get as much as they need from the foods they eat and therefore don't require supplements.

That said, supplemental vitamins and minerals may be needed if your child is a vegetarian, if he eats poorly or has an unusual diet, or if he has an underlying medical condition that interferes with the body's absorption of vitamins and minerals (for example, cystic fibrosis or celiac disease). Supplemental vitamin D is recommended for breast-fed infants. Infants who drink excessive amounts of milk may need additional iron.

Only about one-third of our children have enough calcium in their diets. This means that most of our kids are at risk for bone fractures and, later in life, osteoporosis. Children who drink too much soda and other carbonated beverages are also at risk for poor bone mineralization and osteoporosis.

So what's wrong with just giving your child a multivitamin? Nothing necessarily, as long as you remember that it is a medicine, not a candy. More is not always better. Like all medicines, too much can lead to toxicity! Excessive consumption of some of the water-soluble vitamins probably does nothing more than the recommended amounts, but excessive vitamin C is associated with an increased risk of kidney stones. Fat-soluble vitamins (A, D, E, K) are not excreted in the urine, and consuming too much of these can result in severe toxicity.

The bottom line here is that your children probably don't need daily vitamins if they are eating well-balanced meals. However, there is nothing wrong with a single daily vitamin if you really want to make sure they are getting all of their essential vitamins and minerals. Just limit it to one a day and keep the container in the medicine cabinet out of reach of smaller children. Furthermore, since iron poisoning is a leading cause of toxic ingestion among small children, you may want to choose a multivitamin without iron.

## Tip 15: Beware of food labeling.

Caveat emptor: let the buyer beware. This ageless adage was as true in ancient times as it is these days. In your efforts to raise a healthy eater, you need to be wary of intentionally deceptive food labels bearing marketing buzzwords such as "lite," "low-fat," "70% fat-free," "reduced fat," and so on. What does "reduced fat" mean anyway? Reduced from what? Reduced from a previous version of the product that was even more fattening?

Teach your children to make a habit of reading and interpreting marketing labels and the nutrition labels on packaged products. Have her compare a box of sugary cereal with a more nutritious alternative cereal. Note the deficiencies in the brightly illustrated box of sugar-coated cereal and point out the benefits of the healthier choice. Praise your child for demonstrating these good habits and don't hesitate to sweeten her nutritious cereal with freshly cut strawberries, bananas, blueberries, or other seasonal fruits. If she isn't satisfied with fruit alone, it probably won't hurt her to use artificial sweetening products judiciously.

# CHAPTER 2

# The Basic Rules of Raising a Healthy Eater

*There is obviously more to healthy eating than just understanding the basics of nutrition. Patterns of eating—such as when, where, and how you eat—are habits learned during childhood that can affect your children's future health. Indeed, in my experience I have seen that most children who are obese are eating the wrong foods at the wrong times in the wrong ways. This chapter contains tips that address these issues. Furthermore, there are a few tips meant to help you respond to your child's dietary behavior, thereby enabling you to enact positive change in your family's overall nutritional health.*

## Tip 16
## Acknowledge that your children have their own tastes.

There are four Ps to learn and utilize in raising children, and they are especially useful in regard to pediatric nutrition: personality, patience, positivity, and persistence. I discuss each of these Ps in the next four tips.

Let's start with personality. Keep in mind that though she may be *your* child, your daughter will be her own woman one day; her personality, self-confidence, and tastes are evolving with each new daily experience. Rather than battling at the table over what foods she will eat, encourage her through creative but nonconfrontational techniques to explore her tastes. Here are three techniques that will encourage that kind of exploration while still acknowledging your child's individual tastes:

- Use the **one-bite rule** to ensure that she is exposed to a variety of flavors and textures. Don't expend too much energy preparing elaborate meals for her when she is young. That way you won't be discouraged if she only nibbles at the food on her plate or plays with her food instead of eating it.

- Incorporate **the color game** into meals and snacks so that she will have fun tasting small portions, even just nibbles, of as many naturally colored foods (no M&Ms!) as possible. Praise her for trying new foods and accept that she might not like the taste of them.

- As always, set the tone with **your own good example**. If you or your spouse is a picky eater and refuses to eat vegetables, it's time to grow up and show your children how to be a healthy eater.

## *Tip 17*
## Be patient with your children.

Patience, the second of the four Ps, is a virtue in all walks of life, but nowhere is it more important than with the ones you love. While at times it's hard not to lose your cool when dealing with a small person who has the emotional development of a three-year-old, try to remember that the small person in your care *is* only three!

Getting kids to eat their food—let alone eat healthy food—is one of the challenges in parenting that requires your patience. Rather than flying off the handle because you have prepared an elaborate meal that your child does not appreciate, remind yourself that your child is rejecting the meal, not you. That is, don't take the rejection of your food personally. Attaining this understanding will make your life less stressful and your relationship with your children more rewarding for the years to come.

The best way to remain patient with your child is to share the responsibility with others. A strong network of social support is critical for successful child rearing. If you have family or friends in the area, let them help you out now and then and take a night off from cooking for the kids.

Never shake, slap, smack, or throw your children when you lose your patience! Instead, when you find yourself losing your patience, defuse your anger or frustration by going into another room, turning down the lights, and taking a few quiet minutes to collect yourself. Call a friend immediately if you need help. If you can't do that, or if you don't have a social support network and you find that you cannot calm yourself, every emergency room has a social worker who can help you find resources.

## Tip 18
## Make mealtime a fun and courteous time.

Small children explore the world by interacting with their immediate environment. Often what they are trying to understand ends up in their mouths. Keeping this in mind, you can do yourself a favor, and your children too, by placing age-appropriate foods in front of them and letting them be kids. Things might get messy, but your kids also might enjoy tasting what you put in front of them. As they get a bit older your children will come to appreciate food as something to explore, enjoy, and share with others. Compare the smells and tastes of different types of foods. Discuss what gives foods their color and ask your kids whether they appreciate the texture of the foods they are trying.

Kids love successfully completing tasks! Give them simple chores that they will be able to accomplish, such as setting and clearing the table. This tip brings up another of the four Ps: positivity. Make mealtime a positive experience. Praise your kids for their help. And now that you are teaching them healthy eating habits, you can also teach them polite eating habits. Teach them table manners such as saying "please" and "thank you," chewing with their mouths closed, and talking only with an empty mouth. These habits will make mealtime more pleasant for everyone.

Make mealtime family time. This means no TV, phone calls, or other distractions. Use your dedicated mealtime to talk to your kids and get to know them better.

## Tip 19
## Don't ever give up—gentle persistence will be rewarded.

The Roman poet Ovid wrote, "Let your hook always be cast; in the pool where you least expect it, there will be a fish." This idea brings us to the fourth of the four Ps: persistence. Sure, there are dietary benefits from incorporating, say, fish into your child's diet, but how can you be persistent in the face of your child's obstinate dislike of fish?

It's simple. Just recognize that you don't have to transform your child from a picky eater into one with a taste for all foods. As a parent, you just have to continue to offer her a wide variety of foods on a frequent basis. Eventually, your picky eater will add a few new "likes" to her repertoire. From there, she may begin to try new foods with gusto and, with luck, may one day decide it's more fun to be adventuresome in eating than to be limited.

How many times is too many times to ask a child to try something? There is no right answer. My general feeling is that you shouldn't give up on introducing a food until you've offered it fifteen times. (But don't re-serve the rejected food fifteen meals in a row!) That sounds like a lot of times to prepare something you're pretty sure will be rejected, but if the rest of the family is having the food in question anyway, you need only ask your picky eater to try one bite at each sitting. If you've also limited snacks between meals to ensure that your child is really hungry when he sits down to the meal at which you'll ask him to try a new food, you're more likely to be successful. And don't forget to reward success with praise while staying positive in the face of failure. Be patient and persevere by revisiting past failures. When you least expect it, your child just might take the bait and decide to eat the fish.

## *Tip 20*
## Slowly build a framework for healthy eating.

An ounce of prevention is worth a pound of cure. This is true especially in combating the epidemic of childhood overweight and obesity. Because healthy eating is a lifestyle, it is a lifelong process and one that is best initiated from the beginning of your child's life. You can use the tips in this book to do that. But what about your older children? Don't worry—it's not too late to get started on converting their eating habits and instituting a healthy lifestyle. Get started now!

The first step is to take seriously the need for a healthier, more active lifestyle in order to prevent health problems. This requires that you educate your children and adopt healthy practices for yourself as well. That is, be a good role model. Until you've made healthy eating a part of your own lifestyle, you'll have no credibility when trying to get your kids to change.

It's impossible to tear down your family's old habits and reconstruct a healthy lifestyle all at once. Rome wasn't built in a day. Slowly build a framework for healthy eating for your family. Try achieving small, attainable goals and working toward them until they are reached. This may mean making one food change at a time, such as eating baked instead of fried potato chips. The key is to not change too much at once. Just keep going forward, whatever the pace.

## Tip 21
## Physical activity is part of the foundation of a healthy eating lifestyle.

The key to sustaining a healthy lifestyle is to have a healthy metabolism. The two most important elements toward building a healthy metabolism are healthy eating and physical activity. It's never too early to teach this to your children; the earlier you start, the more of a chance you have to help them develop the attitude that diet and exercise are essential components of a healthy life.

The most common obstacles you face in getting your kids more active are the television, the Internet, and video games. To combat these tempting technologies, it's a good idea to institute "screen time" rules in your house. What does "screen time" mean? It refers to time spent sitting or lying down in front of a monitor or screen of any type, whether television, video game, or computer. Try to set a reasonable limit to the amount of screen time your children get each day. A child's screen time should be less on weekdays and a little more on weekends. Not taking away but simply limiting screen time is an important concept similar to not taking away but limiting certain types of foods to special occasions. Limiting screen time will go far toward getting your kids back onto the playground where they can run, play, and increase their metabolic rates through physical activity.

## *Tip 22*
## Be a positive role model.

More than two-thirds of the obese children I see in my clinic are brought in by obese parents. Because healthy eating is a lifestyle rather than a fad, it needs to be a family affair that is instituted at an early age. The children with the best dental hygiene are those who have made a habit of brushing their teeth at least two times a day for at least two minutes at each brushing. Healthy eating, like regular tooth-brushing, can also be made a habit.

Children resemble you not just because you've given them various combinations of your genes but also because they adopt your mannerisms. Your kids are constantly observing you and modeling their behavior after yours, and they will follow the example you set with your eating. If they observe you overeating, gaining too much weight, and then fad-dieting, they will wrongly assume that this is the appropriate way to eat and live.

Set a dietary example by eating the same foods that you want your children to eat. Keep the quantities of food you eat moderate and choose foods that are low in fat and salt and high in fiber. You set a great example when your children observe that exercise is a part of your daily routine. Remember, teaching your kids to be healthy eaters for life starts with you, so buckle up and get ready for the ride.

## Tip 23
## Don't force your children to eat when they aren't hungry.

Though you might feel embattled, don't draw lines in the sand when it comes to your cooking and your children. To help your children have a positive attitude about eating healthy, don't let dinner become an arena for conflict; this fundamental aspect of your relationship with your child shouldn't become adversarial. Instead, simply provide your children with three well-balanced meals a day and keep in mind that they might eat only one or two complete meals during any given day.

This is normal. If your children are eating one or two full meals a day that you've made sure are packed with nutrients, they probably don't need much at other times. If they complain of already being full at mealtime, however, take a close look at how much milk, Kool-Aid, soda, or juice you've let them have leading up to mealtime. Excess liquids can fill their stomachs, leaving little room for the solids you serve up. If you think this habit might be contributing to your child's decreased appetite at meals, cut back on the milk and juice and see what happens.

Forcing your children to eat when they aren't hungry can lead to feeding problems and even eating disorders in the future. You also shouldn't force your kids to eat more than one bite of foods they don't want. Instead, make meals pleasant and enjoyable and use them as a time to learn about your children's days.

## *Tip 24*
## Make dinner a family affair.

These days the average American household prepares and eats dinner at home fewer than three nights a week. It's tough to squeeze in trips to the grocery store between work, school, ballet lessons, soccer practice, and karate. However, despite the busy schedules of today's families, making time for dinner does not have to be a burden—it just requires planning. Involve your children in planning a menu for the next three or four weeks. If grade school cafeterias can figure it out, so can you. Let your kids help you make the menu and create a grocery list so that shopping can be more efficient and less of a hassle.

Aside from the benefit of eating healthy, a meal eaten together at home can be time spent enjoying your family. Think of the meal preparation time and the sit-down eating time as a down payment on your relationship with your children and on their emotional health. Combine lessons in food preparation, food safety, and manners with quality time. Children like tasks in which they can fully participate and tasks they can see through to completion. After they've washed their hands, get your children involved in the mealtime process by letting them measure and mix ingredients; younger children can set and clear the table. Perhaps most importantly, praise your kids for their contribution to the meal.

## Tip 25
## Limit eating to the table and high chair.

One of the most frequent statements I hear from mothers is, "My child doesn't eat anything!" Yet a review of the child's weight often reveals that the child is at an appropriate weight, or even overweight, despite "never" eating. Furthermore, and too often, the child's face is smeared with crumbs from various chips, crackers, and cookies, and his tongue may range in color from green to purple after recently downing a juicebox. With a little further questioning, we get to the bottom of the real problem: the child doesn't eat anything when the family sits at the table for a meal.

Eating small, frequent meals throughout the day is good advice for your kids if the foods they eat are nutritionally adequate. But a constant infusion of cream-filled chocolate cookies and juice is not the foundation of a healthy diet! Your children will become "full" from eating unhealthy but tasty snacks and have no interest in lunch or dinner if you've stocked the cabinets with this kind of food and given them unlimited access to it. You can't expect your children to have the discipline to refrain from eating such foods if they are readily available.

Snacks that you provide are okay during the day, but sit your children down at the table to eat their snacks so that they develop the habit of doing their eating at the table. This can prevent your kids from getting into the habit of sitting in front of the TV with a bag of potato chips.

## Tip 26
## Even if your kids are picky eaters, don't cook separate meals.

There are many things you can do to encourage your children to enjoy their meals, but one thing you should not do is prepare different meals for them. Your children will not allow themselves to starve, so don't worry if they skip the occasional meal or if they just pick at some of your dishes. You're not a waitress, and your kitchen isn't Denny's, so don't feel that you have to whip up a separate meal for each of your kids. Let's face it: most parents don't have the time or the energy to prepare a separate meal for each member of the family, and you shouldn't feel obliged to.

There are some things that you can do, however, to encourage your children to eat with the family. Include your kids in the weekly or monthly menu planning, but don't allow them to engineer each meal around their one or two favorite foods. You should be aware of your children's favorite dishes and do your best to incorporate them into your menu at least every other week. For typical meals, incorporate familiar and acceptable dishes, but keep in mind that children still need to be exposed to new types of foods. Remember, kids may reject a food more than ten times and then come to like it, so persevere.

## Tip 27
## Do not single out some foods and label them as bad.

The word "diet" has two common usages. As a noun, it simply means what we eat, our "diet." As a verb, "to diet" implies restricting foods, fats, and calories. It's this second use of "diet" that's associated with deprivation and discomfort! The major reason people do not adhere to diets they perceive to be healthy is that these diets often require going without certain "bad" foods. Help your kids steer clear of this difficulty by not labeling foods as "bad." Help them to understand that balance and moderation are the keys to a healthy diet. With a healthy diet, they won't need to diet!

A healthy diet is a healthy eating lifestyle. Your children's healthy diet is like a puzzle, and the foods they eat are the pieces. Each piece fits together to form the whole picture. Some foods may have more protein, fat, or sugar, while others may have more vitamins or fiber. There is a place for all these foods. What makes a diet good or bad is how the foods fit together to form a complete picture.

Balancing the puzzle pieces for your kids is important. They need more than fifty different types of nutrients, vitamins, and minerals every day for good health. Since your child can't get them all from a few select foods, it is important to balance your children's daily choices (along with your own). And since there are no good or bad foods, your family doesn't need to miss out on the foods you all enjoy! The best way to make sure you get the right balance is to eat a wide variety of foods in moderation each day by following the food pyramid guidelines.

## *Tip 28*
## Cut your child's food into small pieces that are easy to chew.

It may seem that this tip would apply only to small children, but people of all ages benefit from this advice. Sure, cutting food into small pieces prevents children from choking on pieces that are too large, but for everyone, cutting food into small pieces has many other benefits as well.

Cutting food into smaller pieces makes it easier to chew it adequately and increases the surface area of the food in the mouth, making it easier for the digestive enzymes present in the mouth, such as amylase, to begin their work. Furthermore, with the food on his plate cut into small pieces, your child will put less into his mouth at a time. Because he'll naturally spend more time eating the meal or snack, satiation will occur and he'll be fully satisfied without having overeaten.

## Tip 29
## Make the push to prepare and eat your dinners earlier.

One of the problems with the way most of us eat, particularly our on-the-go kids, is the pattern of our eating. Skipping breakfast and gorging on high-fat foods at lunchtime leaves us hungry by the time dinner rolls around. Parents are working more hours than ever before, and dinners are often later than they used to be. As a result, families are eating the wrong types of foods at the wrong times!

Do what you can to get your family's eating done before 7:30 P.M. This will allow time for some digestion and utilization of calories to occur before your children go to bed and lie down. Because unused calories are efficiently stored as fat, the calories your child consumes at dinner and does not burn by bedtime just go into making her fatter. Eating earlier will also allow your child to wake up hungry and ready for a nutritious breakfast.

## Tip 30
## Separate screen time from eating time.

You've probably heard it time and time again, but now it's time to listen: don't let your kids eat while they are watching TV. I've already talked about why mealtime should be family time, but just as important, snack times shouldn't be couch potato time. Of course, regardless of where they are consumed, snacks should be nutritious. Snacks that come in wrappers or bags are usually not healthful but instead provide empty, non-nutritious calories that are converted to fat by our bodies.

The more fat, or nonlean body mass, your child has, the lower her metabolic rate becomes. This causes her to burn fewer calories at rest and leads to the efficient deposition of her extra unused calories as additional fat. It is not difficult to see that this generates a vicious cycle of weight gained as fat. Furthermore, the calories obtained while lounging around are not likely to be utilized, since the body burns very few calories while sitting. Consider this: your child can burn four calories per minute while running, and eight calories per minute while swimming, but will burn only about one calorie per minute while watching television. Even reading and thinking hard, however mentally exhausting they may be, burn only one to one and a half calories per minute. At that rate, it's easy to see why couch potatoes have spare tires and love handles.

Do your kids a favor: separate TV time from eating time and encourage them to be active.

## *Tip 31*
## Teach your kids to chew their food thoroughly.

Chewing food is a lot like breathing: many of us do it without ever thinking about it. Here are some ideas, however, to chew on. Chewing their food at least ten times per fork- or spoonful helps prevent your children from choking on food particles too large for their esophagus. Chewing breaks up large particles into smaller bits and lubricates them with saliva. It also slows down the eating process, making it less likely that food will go down the wrong pipe and into the respiratory tree.

Chewing stimulates the secretion of saliva with amylases that begin digestion before food even reaches the stomach. Even the most pureed soups need to be covered in saliva. If you slow down and taste the soup in your mouth before you swallow, the carbohydrates present in the soup can be partially digested by your saliva. Also, by keeping food in the mouth a little longer before swallowing, you allow receptors in your mouth to recognize the nutrients in the meal and send signals to the brain and enteric nervous system, where a plan for digestion is formulated. The correct hormones and enzymes are then released to allow for the nutrients in the meal to be broken down, absorbed, and utilized by the right parts of the body.

Chewing food thoroughly also ensures that meals take longer, allowing your child to feel full before overeating. For your smaller children, you should cut food into smaller pieces and allow them to eat only one or two pieces at a time. This ensures adequate chewing, decreases the risk of choking, and adds time to the meal.

## Tip 32
## Teach your children to adopt a sustainable diet founded on the principle of moderation.

As one Joseph Hall said many years ago, "Moderation is the silken string running through the pearl chain of all virtues" (*Christian Moderation*, 1640).

Sustainability is frequently overlooked by those making lifestyle changes. The key to sustainability is moderation, which makes it easy to sustain a healthy eating lifestyle because your kids won't be deprived of things they like. They will simply learn not to overindulge in them.

Moderation needs to be applied to both your children's eating habits and their activity levels. Moderation in eating means eating a variety of foods and eating them in the right quantities. Eating a few foods to the exclusion of the myriad food choices available makes it harder for kids to get the nutrients they need for growth and development. Eating too much of any food, whether broccoli or chocolate cake, is also not a great idea. Limit serving sizes and make your kids wait twenty minutes before offering a second helping. This will give them time to become full.

Ideally your children should be exercising thirty to sixty minutes a day at least three times a week. Whether that exercise comes in the form of participating in an organized sport or simply running around the yard or biking the neighborhood with friends doesn't matter. Getting less exercise than this is clearly detrimental to their future cardiovascular and musculoskeletal health. However, what about the other extreme? Too much exercise can lead to dehydration, heat stroke, electrolyte imbalances, seizures, and even death. Even before these extremes are reached, muscle and bone injuries occur during prolonged exercise, and muscle breakdown occurs after one and a half to two hours of intense exertion.

If you encourage moderation when it comes to a regimen of physical activity and eating, you will ensure that your kids are able to sustain their habits throughout their lives, maximizing the health benefits of an active lifestyle while minimizing the complications of being overactive.

# Tip 33
## Don't prioritize particular foods on the plate.

Successful people will tell you that prioritizing is the way to accomplish a given task. When it comes to introducing children to new foods, however, parents need to learn what the real priorities are. In the end, it really doesn't matter if your kids won't eat broccoli as long as they are eating lots of other green leafy vegetables. The real priority is to teach your child to be a lifelong healthy eater, not to make sure he finishes the snow peas on his plate.

Your task in this regard is simple. Prepare a well-balanced meal and serve your children small portions. Introduce a new food a couple of times a week, but do not prioritize foods on the plate. Adhere to the one-bite rule, and if your child decides not to eat all of a new food, don't despair. He might not like it right away or even anytime soon. Many tastes are acquired over time, and your child might start eating a previously rejected food after the twentieth time you offer it.

Keep a positive attitude and be persistent, but also be consistent by adhering to the principles of the food pyramid when preparing and serving snacks and meals. Each part of the meal is supplying needed nutrients and energy, so don't make one dish more important than the others.

## Tip 34
## Give teens increased food independence.

Parents sometimes need to be reminded that adolescence is difficult and that older children and young adults are appropriately battling to find out who they are and where they fit in. They want to make choices on their own, but at the same time they are not always ready to handle the responsibilities that go along with those choices.

As might be expected, younger teens need more help in making decisions than older ones. As she gets older, and with practice, your child will become better able to weigh and understand the possible consequences of her behaviors, but this will happen only if you allow her to make decisions. Making personal food choices is a great way to practice making responsible decisions. This doesn't mean you should agree to throw the food pyramid out the window and serve up burgers and fries every night. Initially offer reasonable and healthful foods from which she can decide what she wants to eat. If you have laid a solid foundation for healthy eating and living centered on activity, moderation at mealtime, and variety, the transition to making her own decisions will be smoother.

Most arguments between parents and children are about everyday things or differences in personal tastes and choices, not about serious differences in values. Don't let food choices become a barrier between you and your child.

## Tip 35
## Offer your children smaller serving sizes at mealtime.

Were we ever satiated in the days before supersizing? I don't recall ever going to bed hungry, yet the trend for most Americans has been to eat larger servings at each meal. Some people don't stop eating until they have to unbutton their pants. This might be okay for Thanksgiving Day, but it shouldn't be the way you teach your children to eat day in and day out. In addition to watching what your kids eat, trim down how much they eat with each serving.

Attempt to serve smaller portions of foods that are high in starch and fiber and only small helpings of fatty foods, such as cheese and high-fat meats. Cut your children's food into smaller pieces and make sure they are chewing their food thoroughly before swallowing. Encourage conversation at the dinner table, but only with an empty mouth. These practices make dinner take a bit longer and allow your kids time to feel satiated by what they have eaten. If you make your kids wait twenty to thirty minutes before second helpings, they are more likely to be satisfied with their meal and ready for a healthy dessert.

## Tip 36
## Limit your children's consumption of unhealthy snacks and sugary drinks.

There is room for nearly every type of food in your diet as long as high-fat foods do not become the staple foods that are eaten daily. Too often children obtain far too many empty calories every single day from non-nutritious but high-fat sources such as fried snacks and sugar-filled drinks.

When educating parents, I've borrowed a slogan from one of my colleagues: limit the "-os" in your kids' diets. This means cut back on purchasing and feeding your kids foods and snacks that end in "-os": Fritos, Doritos, Tostitos, burritos, Spaghettios, Oreos, and Cheetos! It's simplistic, but parents usually get the point. The "-os" rule isn't meant to single out the products that end in "-os" but to remind parents to limit all fried chips, baked crackers, cookies, snack cakes, juices, and nondiet sodas in their children's diets. Most parents wouldn't serve a dinner of Pringles, and yet most of their kids' calories may be coming from non-nutritive chips, crackers, cakes, and soda.

Unhealthy snacking will, at the extreme, lead to obesity. Fast food, unhealthy snacks, and sodas are the unholy trinity of childhood obesity and the arsenal of what one of my mentors calls "carbo-lipo-terrorism." Childhood obesity, which can lead to heart disease, diabetes, strokes, and other problems for your kids later in life, has reached epidemic proportions. In the meantime, unhealthy snacking causes children to have poor appetites at meals. When kids fill up on snacks in between meals, they are less likely to try new, healthy foods at mealtime and more likely to become picky eaters.

Stock healthy snacks in the pantry and encourage your children to drink water. If you find it difficult to stop purchasing soda, switch to diet. Save chips, cookies, and cakes for weekends or special occasions. These few simple changes will go a long way to ensuring your children's future eating health.

## Tip 37
## Don't use food or snacks to
## distract children or to keep them busy.

When your small baby cries, it isn't always because she's hungry. Sometimes she just wants to be held. Nonetheless, if you put a sweet-tasting bottle of juice in her mouth, you might just make her stop crying. Good, right? Wrong. Don't start the vicious cycle of associating boredom, sadness, or anxiety with food.

As your baby grows into a toddler she will have an arsenal of energy and curiosity. This can make running errands both in and out of the house difficult. It is tempting to still your child with a sweet snack, but resist the temptation. It's true that your toddler or young child might be cranky because she is hungry and needs a snack. In that case, offer her a nutritious snack, either one that you have prepared in advance or something easy to eat on the go but nutritious as well, like fruit or nuts. However, if your child is cranky because she is tired or bored, don't hand over a snack to occupy her time. If you do, you will be reinforcing in her a bad habit of eating when she has nothing to do or feels bad about something.

Instead of sticking a lollipop in her mouth when she gets fidgety, give her a coloring book and some crayons. Let her use her energy and develop creativity in positive ways instead of trying to distract her with non-nutritive calories from juice or unhealthy snacks.

## *Tip 38*
## Don't punish your children for rejecting certain foods.

Children should be encouraged to try new foods on a regular basis, and you should try hard to enforce the one-bite rule at meals. However, you should also respect your kids' tastes when they have tried something and they tell you they don't like it.

There are many reasons why kids reject foods. Sometimes they are simply mimicking an older sibling or playmate and their aversion has nothing to do with the food's texture, color, smell, or taste. This is very common with younger children, who look up to their older siblings and copy their eating behaviors. Your best chance for success in this case is to enlist your older child's cooperation and help in encouraging the younger child to try new foods, for the sake of their little sibling's health.

Sometimes kids reject a food because they experience mild discomfort when eating it. Especially with milk, egg, fish, or peanut-containing products, your child may be rejecting the food you're offering because she has a mild allergy to it.

Punishing your kids for not liking foods leads to strife at meals and unhealthy food associations that can strain the relationship between you and your kids and foster unhealthy patterns of eating. Instead, simply ask your child to try one bite. He may never want more than that one bite, but you'll have set a consistent standard for behavior at your table.

***Tip 39***
## Set a reasonable pace for change.

Healthy changes in your children's dietary habits will benefit them now and over their lifetimes. Nonetheless, instituting too many changes at once can be disruptive to your
family and lead to failure. Think of adopting a healthy eating and activity regimen as a marathon, not a sprint. Sure,
you can change fifty things at once, but you and your kids
will poop out with exhaustion, much as if you tried to run
as fast as you could for too long a distance. Set a reasonable
pace for your family, and as long as they are making
progress, don't be discouraged if the changes are taking
place slowly.

As a general rule, try changing a maximum of two dietary and activity-level rules every other week. Let your family get used to things before making additional changes. For
instance, start by stocking healthier foods in the cabinets instead of high-fat, caloric snack foods and limiting your children's screen time to one to two hours of television, video
games, and Internet on school nights. These are just a few
simple changes that can take time to be fully accepted by
your family but will pay huge dividends to their health in
the long run.

# CHAPTER 3

# Troubleshooting for Picky Eaters

*All of us know how frustrating it can be to get kids to eat something that they are sure they won't like—or that they are sure they* don't *like! The seemingly futile task of teaching small children to eat a varied diet that includes vegetables is an admittedly difficult but necessary part of raising a healthy eater. In addition to following the basic rules outlined in the tips in chapter 2, you may find the following tips helpful when your picky eaters are being their most picky.*

## Tip 40
# Institute a one-bite rule in your household.

Many dietitians, nurses, and pediatricians have found that picky eaters can be won over to new and interesting foods by employing a trick of the trade called the "one-bite rule." It is as simple as the name implies: you simply ask that your child try one single bite of the new food you're introducing.

By the time this rule can be applied—namely, to your toddlers and young children—they have already acquired a simple set of tastes. Don't blitz them with tangy foods or mixed dishes. Keep things simple and introduce one food at a time. You'll be the most successful if you introduce new foods on days when your kids are the most hungry, so plan ahead and engineer their hunger! More specifically, omit snacking during the afternoon between lunch and dinner for best results.

Explain to your child that it is okay to not like something, but that it is important to try it before making up his mind. Most importantly, reinforce his cooperative behavior and give him lots of praise when he takes that bite. And make sure you and your spouse are following the one-bite rule yourselves. If you don't like something, say so and then explain your reasons. This sets a good model for your children.

In its simplest terms, the one-bite rule just means everyone in the family needs to try at least one bite of a new food. If your child doesn't want more, accept his decision. Have him pick out a new vegetable at the store to try. You may not like it, but let him try it anyway, since he might like it. Use a cookbook to find recipes to make it more exciting even for you. Don't be discouraged or show signs of disappointment when your child declines a second bite. Accept his decision, acknowledging his cooperation in trying the new food. Don't forget to try again later, again and again.

## *Tip 41*
## Pull out all the tricks.

When I was a child, I was as picky an eater as they came. However, my mother had one trick that worked on me every time. She purchased a plastic plate with a picture on it of robots battling in space. I loved that plate. My mother didn't serve my meals from that plate every night but saved it for those nights when she was going to pull eggs, fish, or broccoli on me. I still don't like broccoli, but I'll still eat it if it's served off that plate!

You don't have to limit yourself to purchasing silly—or in that case, very cool—dishware. The point is to make meals fun. Kids like variety, whether we are talking about the color, taste, or texture of foods. Why not give your toddler a piece of paper and a crayon to doodle with during dinner? The distraction could be helpful, and he may also be encouraged to draw what he does and doesn't like.

Also, try giving your dishes funny names. Who can resist sparkleberry soup? Let your kids come up with the funny names and make sure you obediently call the dish by the name they bestow upon it. The only rule is that they have to taste the food to name it. Another tip in my mother's bag of tricks on days when she wanted me to try a new food was to not let me snack between lunch and dinner. That way I was hungry enough to eat anything—as long as it was on the right plate!

## Tip 42
## Don't throw out the rules with your toddler—make the rules flexible so she will succeed.

The toddler years can be messy and frustrating for parents, but instead of focusing on those negative aspects, take an understanding perspective. Toddlers lack the fine motor co-ordination to use a fork or spoon without making a mess. Sometimes they resort to using their hands to eat. They tend to spit, throw, or squash foods, talk with their mouths full, and fidget. Are they intentionally trying to thwart you? Not at all. Toddlers explore the world of food colors, tastes, and textures with both their hands and their mouths. Neverthe-less, it is not a waste of time to begin teaching them how to eat healthy.

Plan for the mess by putting a plastic sheet under the high chair. When your child throws food, gently say "no," but don't pick up the food until the meal is over. Don't turn food-throwing into a game where she throws and you fetch. Offer a variety of food at meals but keep the portions on her plate at any one time small. You are less likely to worry if a couple of small pieces of food hit the floor rather than a whole bowl of food.

Sit your child down for meals at the table or in the high chair as a habit. Toddlers are inquisitive and would prefer to eat and explore, making a mess in the process. You should be patient and understanding but firm, realizing that eating while walking and running can increase your small child's risk for choking.

It's better to not force your child to finish everything on his plate. It is better to waste a few leftovers than battle with your children or force them to eat when they've had enough. Keep in mind that toddlers can recognize their hunger and fullness signals and, unlike adults, don't go on hunger strikes. For reassurance about your child's development, however, ask your pediatrician to review his growth and height charts at your next visit.

Simple rewards may reinforce your child's good behavior. I would suggest being effusive in your compliments when your children demonstrate appropriate table etiquette. You might also offer stickers or hand stamps as a reward, but never use food as a reward: that can lead to unhealthy habits in the future. As always, be a good role model. If your kids see you eating in front of the television between meals, they rightfully won't understand why they shouldn't.

## Tip 43
## Camouflage vegetables in foods
## your kids will eat.

Vegetables are an irreplaceable part of a healthy, balanced
diet, providing fiber, vitamins, and minerals. Every parent
knows this. What most parents also know is that kids generally don't like vegetables! This doesn't mean kids won't eat
them, however, especially if they don't know they're eating
them. Try hiding vegetables in foods they will eat. In this
case, what your kids don't know won't hurt them. In fact,
it'll be good for them.

Soup is an excellent way to provide a variety of nutrients
in one bowl. Adding vegetables such as broccoli, zucchini,
and cauliflower to soups and stews increases their nutritional value. Pureeing vegetables to a soupy consistency in a
blender is a good way to "hide" vegetables from picky eaters
and add color and texture to soups.

Another way to hide vegetables is to include them in familiar favorites such as meatloaf and hamburgers. Your kids
may complain that it isn't McDonald's, but they'll probably
still eat it. You can layer yams, beets, or green beans into
casseroles and lasagna. Finally, serve vegetable sticks with
crackers, cheeses, and fruit. Your kids may not be eating
only vegetables, but getting a picky eater to eat some vegetables is better than watching him eat none at all.

## Tip 44
## Some children prefer softened vegetables.

I've listened to many parents complain that their kids stubbornly refuse to eat vegetables at all. Some of the fault, however, lies with the parents and their previous dietary choices. After all, why would a child accustomed to bottle after bottle of sweet juice want to eat cauliflower when it's introduced? A two-year-old doesn't understand the nutritional benefits of a well-balanced diet—he only knows that purple tastes good! Other parents allow their kids to fill up on non-nutritious snacks before meals, leaving no room for foods at mealtime. The good news is that many of these "picky eaters" can be reformed with a little planning and preparation.

We all have certain foods that we like or dislike because of the texture or color rather than the flavor or smell. This is particularly true of toddlers and small children. Making the transition from pureed foods to chewable solids can be a rough period for parents. Previously "good" eaters can become picky. Part of the problem is that the new foods are different in consistency and texture from the foods to which they were accustomed. When making this switch, serve soft fruits such as bananas, peaches, and pears. Steam vegetables until they are soft, even mushy. If this doesn't work, puree vegetables into a soup. You might lose some of the minerals from oversteaming vegetables such as broccoli, but your child will still get the fiber from them and will begin to eat the previously rejected food. As she gets older she will learn to appreciate crisper produce, but for the time being try to be content that she is eating a healthy, varied diet.

## *Tip 45*
## Younger children tend to like plain foods.

As complex as human development and physiology are, your young children are actually rather simple creatures. They need love, attention, directed stimulation, food, and sleep. They like their books filled with pictures and pop-outs, their television programs bright and filled with songs, and their food bland and easy to eat.

Your children will rapidly become more sophisticated in their literature, music, and food tastes, but don't push them. Children resist trying new foods that are too spicy or ones they can't identify. Avoid mixed dishes such as casseroles and instead stick to plain dishes that are easily identifiable, such as macaroni. Advance your child to macaroni and cheese, then add some pepper. Don't be afraid to push the envelope, just don't push your kid over the edge.

## Tip 46
# Make meals and snacks colorful and nutritious.

Colors in foods have no inherent nutritional value, but the natural color of certain foods may give clues to the nutrients contained within them. A visit to any produce section reveals that fruits and vegetables, besides being loaded with the important vitamins and minerals necessary for your growing children, come in myriad colors.

Children like contrasting colors, so incorporate this idea into their meals. When coloring, few kids go straight for the brown crayon, so why should you limit their meals to beef and french fries? Playing the color game is a great way to encourage small children to eat vegetables. The game is simple. See who can take a few bites of the most colors on the table. Everybody wins when your kids eat a variety of fruits and vegetables, even if they are only taking a few bites of each.

The healthful benefits of playing the color game are numerous. Sampling small portions of vegetables adds time to the meal, allowing satiation to occur before children overeat. It also provides fiber in your child's diet, preventing constipation. The only limitation to the color game is your imagination. Top green salads with fresh fruit like peaches and tangerines or with raisins. Stir various fruits and vegetables into pasta salads or create fruit salads using a variety of fruit such as bananas, kiwis, peaches, plums, grapes, oranges, and strawberries.

# *Tip 47*
# Plan a taste test challenge.

We all remember the days of the Coke-Pepsi taste tests, and most of us will admit to pulling out the blindfolds for our own home-based taste tests. In addition to putting to rest which soda tasted better, we had fun! This tip is one I pulled out of my mother's bag of tricks. If she knew that I would eat anything served on my robot plate, she also knew that my brother would eat anything in the context of a taste test.

You can fashion a blindfold out of any opaque material in your home, such as the cloth belt of a shower robe, or you can make a mask out of construction paper and string. Just don't put a bag over your child's head! Next, prepare two new vegetables—or two vegetables prepared in a different way—and one at a time match them up against another vegetable that you know your child will eat. Be very formal about the contest. Your child is the "official food-testing judge" and should be offered a drink between bites to cleanse his palate. The more you immerse your family into the game of taste-testing, the more successful the outcome will be.

Keep in mind, however, that even though your child will have fun taste-testing, not everything will taste good to him. The goal, however, is simply to have him follow the one-bite rule by taking that one bite!

## *Tip 48*
## Take your kids on a supermarket scavenger hunt.

Trips to the grocery store don't have to be painful for you or your young ones. In fact, you can make your weekly or monthly trips to the store into fun for the whole family. After creating a healthy shopping list, divvy it up into smaller scavenger hunt lists for your children.

When your kids are still very young and not yet reading, you can lead them down the aisle and let them "help" you find nonbreakable items, such as cardboard boxes of macaroni. Once your children are old enough to read, you can allow them to find items in the supermarket on their own. Reward your children with effusive praise for accomplishing their tasks, and when you get home, enlist their cooperation in tasting each of the items they helped to locate.

Besides making the chore of food shopping fun and interactive for your kids, the scavenger hunt strategy has the added and long-lasting benefit of interesting your kids in food and in food labels. Of course, it also allows them to feel needed and responsible, and in that frame of mind they may be more interested in helping you cook and in tasting your creations!

# CHAPTER 4

# Meals, Snacks, and Beverages

*In the preceding chapters, the tips have focused on the basics of nutrition and on building a framework for successfully raising a healthy eater. This chapter gives more specific tips on what to eat and when to eat, including some recipes that are among my favorite recommendations. In addition to focusing on specific meals, some of the tips focus on holiday eating, eating out, kitchen hygiene, and meal planning.*

## Tip 49
## Healthy eating starts with breakfast.

Race car drivers always begin the race on a full tank of gas. For many of the same reasons, your child should start his day the same way. Eating breakfast is the pre-race pit stop you should make sure your child takes. Indeed, breakfast is widely regarded as the most important meal of the day because it breaks the overnight fasting period, replenishes your child's supply of glucose, and provides other essential nutrients to keep his energy level up throughout the day.

Glucose, the body's energy source, is broken down and absorbed from the carbohydrates we eat, and it accounts for around 0.1% of our blood volume. By the time morning rolls around, our bodies have gone without food for as long as twelve hours, causing our glucose levels, or blood sugar, to drop. When this happens, our bodies compensate by releasing the glucose stored in our muscle tissue and liver, called glycogen. Once all of the energy from the glycogen stores is used up, the body breaks down fatty acids to produce energy. But fatty acids cannot be converted into glucose, so some body protein from muscle has to be broken down and converted to glucose to get the body's necessary fuel.

Some of the essential vitamins, minerals, and other nutrients can be gained only from food, not from stored glucose. So even though your body can usually find enough energy to make it to the next meal, it's not a good idea to let a body—least of all a growing body—steal resources from itself to find energy for the day. Around one in eight American children skip breakfast. "Going without" becomes more common with advancing age: approximately 15% of teenagers and one-third of adults don't eat breakfast. Just as the racer who starts the race with half a tank of gas must stop to refuel (thereby allowing other racers to pass), children and adults who go without breakfast demonstrate diminished energy levels and decreased ability to concentrate at school and work, with resulting decreases in performance.

One study found that schoolchildren who don't eat breakfast have much lower levels of iron, zinc, dietary fiber, calcium, and vitamin $B_2$ than children who do take the time to have breakfast. It appears that refueling with lunch, dinner, and snacks isn't sufficient to make up the nutritional deficit and provide full energy levels or performance. Other studies suggest a link to obesity in those who regularly skip breakfast. Compared to children who regularly eat breakfast, those who skip breakfast tend to consume fewer calories overall and yet they experience slightly higher rates of overweight and obesity! People who skip breakfast are usually ravenous by lunchtime and tend to eat more of the wrong types of foods to compensate.

Given all this, do what's necessary in your morning routine to make sure your child gets nutritious food and the time to eat it. While you're at it, change your own routine and make breakfast a part of your morning scramble as well.

## Tip 50
## Encourage your children to eat healthy at school.

So you always try to cook healthy and you limit screen time in front of the TV, the computer, and video games to one to two hours on school days, but your child is still overweight. How can this be? It must mean he's just genetically programmed to be fat, right? Wrong. The answer often lies in a detailed dietary history. First of all, what does he eat in the morning before school? Well, nothing—he's too rushed to eat breakfast. Okay. What does he eat for lunch? I don't know. I give him five dollars to buy his lunch at school.

What's happening here? Part of the answer is right in front of you. After skipping breakfast, your child is ravenous by the time lunch rolls around, and the five dollars you gave him in the morning for breakfast can go either toward a well-balanced, government-approved, boring meal with a carton of milk from the lunch line or toward a cheeseburger, bag of chips, piece of pie, and soda from the snack bar.

You can't be with your child at all times, but you can ensure that he eats breakfast before school, and you can encourage him to eat healthy at school by setting a good example in the meals you eat together. Furthermore, you can buy a meal ticket for your younger children and get them into the habit of eating the nutritionally appropriate and balanced "government-issued" school food.

## Tip 51
## Make fun-packed lunches for your small children.

It doesn't matter if you're running errands around town or sending your kids off to school—pack a healthy lunch for them. Your lunches are competing with fast food and whatever the other kids have in their lunch boxes. When your kids are at school and out of sight, you can be sure that they will be tempted by their friends' store-bought snack packs. Many of these snacks, despite their enticing packaging, are not as healthful as they should be. It's simple but true: there is no substitute for a healthy, well-balanced meal that you've packed yourself.

That said, there are things you can do to make your child's home-packed lunch interesting and perhaps even the envy of her peers. When I was small, I was the king of picky eaters and wouldn't go near a box of cereal whose contents weren't completely sugar-coated. My mother discovered, however, that I would eat less sugary cereals if they had a prize in the box. Soon she was busy rigging the event, placing stickers and other small prizes in the boxes of healthy cereals.

You can purchase stickers and inexpensive party-favor-style toys and try the same trick in your child's lunch box. Pop a toy in with her carrot sticks and she will come to look forward to veggies with lunch! Perhaps the most important aspect of this tip is to communicate with your child's teacher. Find out what your child is eating for lunch. Is she eating her carrots or just playing with the little toy you packed with them? Cooperation with her teacher will allow you to maximize her nutrition and to stay well informed.

## Tip 52
## All your child needs to drink during the first year of life is breast milk or formula.

There was a time—and indeed, many a family still subscribes to the idea—when infants and babies were given juice, water (or sugar water), or tea in addition to breast milk or formula. Though in moderation (four to eight ounces a day at most) most of these liquids will do little damage (tea can cause seizures even in small quantities), the nutritional truth is that the only liquid your baby needs during the first year of life is breast milk or formula. Each is mostly water—which your baby very much needs—but also contains the precious electrolytes that a growing baby needs.

One of the problems with giving alternative fluids is that, to develop normally, your growing baby needs nutrients that are largely missing from fluids other than breast milk and formula, such as amino acids from proteins, fatty acids from fat, and calories from carbohydrates. And of course, the long-range issue with turning your kids on to juice at a young age is that they will become juice-a-holics as they grow from infant to toddler. This can result in damage to their developing teeth and obesity with its associated problems.

## *Tip 53*
## Get off the bottle ASAP, but not too early.

A very common pediatric issue is that of weaning from the bottle. You might be wondering, what's the big deal? Why can't your daughter suck on a bottle until she's twelve? In addition to the social embarrassment and harassment she might face if she showed up for preschool with a bottle, there are a couple of other reasons to get off the bottle as soon as possible.

Some children who are not breast-fed develop a bottle dependency that can lead to cavities and malformed dentition. This is a particular risk for babies who are put to bed with a bottle. The longer you do this with your baby, the harder it will be when you pull the rug out from under him. The best thing is to never start the habit of going to bed with a bottle. Toddlers who spend the whole day intermittently sucking on bottles can also develop tooth decay and improperly formed teeth. One last problem is that children older than one year old are probably drinking cow's milk. Too much cow's milk can displace other nutrient-rich foods from the diet and can also lead to anemia.

The healthy alternative to letting your child have a bottle all day or when going to bed is to offer her the bottle only at the table and then only for a twenty- to thirty minute period. Your child will quickly come to expect that this is the time to drink her milk or formula and will indeed drink it at that time.

You'll know it's time to wean your child from the bottle when she is capable of drinking from a sippy cup. Your child will gradually signal that she is ready to drink from a cup. She should have the coordination to sit up unassisted and be tolerating pureed foods well. Start offering assisted sips at around six months. Initially she will still be getting most of her milk from the bottle or the breast, but by around eight to ten months she should be able to drink from a sippy cup alone. Sometime between ten and eighteen months your child should have mastered these tasks and be ready to get off the bottle.

When the day comes to let the bottle go, there is no looking back. Throw all of the bottles in the trash. You should expect anywhere from a couple of days to a week of crying. The longer you wait, the longer the outcry will last. For parents who have exclusively breast-fed without pumping, don't introduce bottles at all. Go straight from mom's breast to a sippy cup.

## Tip 54
## Change the way your family snacks.

These days more than 95% of the adults and children in this country have at least one snack each day. Many common snack foods are high in salt, fat, sugar, and calories. If your children regularly make unhealthy snack choices, the effect on their health will be negative. That's the bad news, but the good news is that snacks can be good for your children if you teach them to make healthy choices.

Children often cannot eat enough at three meals a day to satisfy their hunger and provide all of the nutrients they need. Snacks can supplement the calories they get from meals and provide the other nutrients they need to grow and develop normally. The best way to ensure that your children snack wisely is to plan snacks as a part of the day's menu. Let your children choose from snacks they helped pick out from the store, such as fruits, vegetables, and low-fat crackers and low-fat cheeses. Avoid caloric, fat-filled, or salty snacks such as candy, chips, and soda. Offer snacks at regular times and do strive to limit snacks to these times only. If you offer a snack at midmorning and again at midafternoon—times I recommend—you'll be best able to control what your kids are eating and to make sure that they don't think of snacks as foods that are available to them all day long.

## Tip 55
## Prepare pre-portioned snacks for your school-age children.

As the average parents work more and more hours per week, keeping the refrigerator and cabinets stocked with healthy foods can be a demanding task—demanding, but not impossible. It just takes a little planning, and it's important enough to try to make a little time for. After all, we can't expect our children to make healthy food decisions if we don't supply them with healthy food choices!

When children come home from school, they inevitably go in search of a midafternoon snack. Anticipate this and pre-pack snacks for the home cabinet just as you would for your younger children's school lunches. Small children like having their own designated snacks, and you can be assured they are eating healthy because you packed the snack yourself. Instead of just one type of snack, pack an assortment of goodies. Each portion should be small. A few crackers, a few chips, some celery sticks or carrot sticks, and so on. The important thing with small children is that you provide them with variety. Just as when packing lunches, putting a sticker or something small in the pack provides positive encouragement for your child. (Remember, children choose cereal for the prize in the box!)

These pre-packed snacks are also great for when you are out and about performing your errands. Taking a healthy snack along will keep you from having to buy your kids fast food to handle their mood swings, which may be driven by hunger.

## Tip 56
## Offer your children choices when planning meals and snacks.

Have you ever noticed that crayon sets for the smallest children come in boxes of four or five while boxes meant for older kids have as many as one hundred crayons in them? Children need to develop a framework for success whether they are coloring or eating. Younger kids accept their four colors while they are still learning to color within the lines, but as they master these basic skills they grow to crave variety.

Of course, children of all ages need variety and a balanced diet, but smaller kids accept that you, their parent, are the one to decide what colors will be in their crayon box or what food will be on their plate. As they get older, however, start involving your kids in the decisionmaking process. This doesn't mean giving your eight-year-old twenty dollars and setting him loose in the grocery store. If you do that, you shouldn't be surprised if he selects twenty dollars' worth of snack cakes! What this *does* mean is that you should give your child options—healthy options—and let him choose from them. Do you want peas, green beans, or broccoli tonight? Do you want rice or potatoes? Would you like strawberries for dessert or watermelon? Offering your children choices encourages them to eat what you are preparing and makes them feel that you care about their preferences and desires.

## Tip 57
## Encourage your children to eat salads with meals.

The benefits of eating salads with meals are numerous. First, the obvious: salad can be a rich source of vitamins, minerals, and fiber. It also contains antioxidants that have anticancer properties in addition to other health benefits. A salad provides fiber, helping to prevent constipation. A green salad or fruit salad is also a great way to achieve the minimum recommended servings for fruits and vegetables.

Another plus is that having a salad with a meal adds eating time to the meal. More time means that everyone has a chance to feel full before they overeat.

If you're in a hurry, today's pre-made salads in bags are great. Just open, rinse, and eat.

Remember: salads in and of themselves are low-calorie, but when you drench a salad in a high-fat or high-sugar dressing, you are canceling out the benefits. See the next tip for healthier salad dressing ideas.

## Tip 58
## Keep salads healthy.

Eating vegetables and salads is healthy. And it seems that we're all getting that message loud and clear: salad consumption is at an all-time high. More than two-thirds of American households report serving salads at least once a day, according to the USDA. Unfortunately, the same report indicated that children who eat salads obtain as much fat or more from salad dressing as from any other food source. After adding salad dressing, croutons, cheese, bacon bits, egg, and anything else that tastes good but is not so good for us, a salad can end up being higher in fat and calories than a meal of potato chips and chocolate chip cookies!

So what can you do to keep up the flavor so as to encourage children to eat salads at all? Regular dressing can be high in calories and fat, and very often salads are drenched in it, so when eating out, ask for dressing on the side and use only one to one and a half tablespoons.

The choice of dressing is also important. Try switching to a low-fat or fat-free dressing. Believe it or not, your kids will actually like some of them. Mix balsamic vinegar with honey-mustard for a homemade low-calorie dressing. You can also make fat-free, low-cal dressing from fat-free, sugar-free yogurt mixed with fat-free ranch powder purchased by the pack from your grocery store.

## Tip 59
## Avoid high-fat add-ons.

Certain foods eaten every day lead inexorably to a larger waistline, obesity, and the related diseases that afflict the obese. A daily regimen of hamburgers, french fries, soda, and ice cream for dessert is clearly not healthful. This doesn't mean that these foods can't be eaten occasionally. The current food pyramid recommendations refer to foods at the base of the pyramid as "everyday foods" and the foods at the very top of the pyramid as "sometime foods." Hamburgers with french fries, soda, and ice cream clearly fall into the "sometime" category.

But what constitutes "sometime"? Can these occasional meals be once a week, twice a week, or twice a month? It depends, but don't use the idea of "sometime" meals to give your children carte blanche for gluttony. If your kids want to have more than one or two burgers during the week, make them as healthy as possible. You can do this by avoiding the high-fat add-ons. Avoid adding cheese, gobs of mayo, and fat-soaked bacon to the burger. On the other hand, if your kids eat a burger only once or twice a month, maybe it isn't so bad to load it up once in a while. Use common sense. Just remember that the decisions you make for your children's diets now will affect their health in the future.

## Tip 60
# Veggies are veggies, whether fresh or frozen.

Most of us don't have time to buy, clean, and cook fresh fruits and vegetables daily. Even still, that shouldn't be a reason not to serve fruits and vegetables to your children. Although my wife will tell you that she can taste the difference between fresh and frozen fruits and vegetables, doctors and nutritionists will tell you they are virtually identical in nutritional content. In fact, if you live in areas where fresh produce is shipped in from long distances or stored for a long time before being consumed, frozen and canned produce is likely to be higher in nutritional content because fresh produce can lose nutrients over time and through exposure to heat.

This is true if you are comparing a fresh fruit salad to fruit cocktail canned in the fruit's own juices. However, beware of fruits canned in heavy syrup or creamed versions of vegetables. With these food products, you may be consuming unwanted fat and calories. Also beware of canned produce with added sodium. These products will add unwanted fat, calories, and salt to your diet.

## Tip 61
## Cut down on fat and salt by seasoning with herbs and spices.

Oils and salt are responsible for much of the added flavor we crave in our foods. Unfortunately, when eaten in excess, as they often are in our society, they also contribute to or exacerbate heart disease and hypertension. That said, you don't have to eliminate oils and salt from your cooking entirely to eat healthy. Just cut back on the salt and oils you add while you cook and see if your kids still enjoy the food. Chances are they won't even notice the change you've made in the name of healthful cooking.

If you or your children do miss the oils and salt you used to put into your meals, step up the flavor of your family's dishes by adding spices and herbs such as pepper, oregano, thyme, basil, or rosemary. Fresh or dried doesn't really matter, but if you have the space to grow herbs and spices in your yard (or on a windowsill), you can enlist your kids in the harvesting of them. This gives your kids a job to do in the kitchen while you cook, and their being involved in meal preparation is good for everyone in the family.

## Tip 62
## Eating out can be fun *and* healthy.

Some families eat out more often than they eat at home. Though it might be a little harder on your wallet, eating out or bringing in take-out food doesn't have to be unhealthy. As a rule of thumb, stick to the main concepts of healthful eating that you would apply to a home-cooked meal. More specifically, understand that the larger portions served in most restaurants are a marketing ploy and usually provide far more food than you or your children need to eat. So don't encourage your kids to eat everything on their plates when eating out. Instead, encourage them to eat only about as much as they would at home. There is nothing wrong with taking leftovers home and having them the next day.

Another reason restaurant food tastes so good is that they don't hesitate to add oil for flavor. (This is another marketing ploy to get you to come back.) Be on the lookout for high-fat and saucy foods. Instead of fried foods, order foods that are broiled, boiled, steamed, grilled, or baked.

Another way to eat healthy when eating out is to start your meal—and your kids'—with a salad. Salads add fiber to your kids' diets and helps prevent them from overeating. Don't worry that they won't be able to finish the meal you've paid for. If they're full, be content. Just be careful not to make your salad unhealthy with gobs of dressing, cheese, bacon bits, and oily croutons. And one last little tip that'll go a long way toward staying healthy when eating out: instead of ordering individual desserts, order just one or two for the whole family to share.

## Tip 63
## Teach your children the principles of safe and sanitary food handling.

Even healthful foods can be unhealthy if they are not handled and prepared correctly. Most of us know that eggs and chicken can transmit salmonella and that beef can transmit E. coli, but people often forget that it is possible to contract the same bacterial infections from fresh produce. These bacteria get on our fruits and vegetables in a couple of ways. Sometimes the manure used as fertilizer is contaminated with bacteria that can adhere to the surfaces of the produce. Sometimes the bacteria find their way onto our foods from the hands of food handlers and grocers. In addition to ridding your food of bacteria, you should wash your fresh fruit and vegetables to get rid of pesticides that may still be clinging to them.

Here are some other tips for handling and preparing food properly:

- Bacteria on a steak will be killed if the surface is browned, but ground beef must be fully cooked throughout to be sterilized.

- Do not use the same utensils and plates for cooked food that you used to prepare and store it.

- Kitchen sponges should be disposed of after a few weeks, and kitchen rags washed regularly.

- Use plastic and glass cutting boards rather than wooden cutting boards to decrease the transmission of bacteria to your foods.

- Finally, wash your hands before, during, and after food preparation. This is not only protective but also instills hygienic habits in both you and your children.

## Tip 64
**Teach your children to cook.**

It is important to include your children in meal preparation when they are young. Doing so is a great way to introduce them to a variety of food flavors and textures as well as to teach them kitchen safety, basic cooking techniques, and lessons on healthy eating. Another plus: your kids are more likely to try something they helped prepare than something that's just dished out to them.

Smaller kids, age three to six, should be able to add ingredients to a bowl and stir them; they can also wash fresh produce. Seven- to nine-year-olds should be able to use measuring cups and spoons, an electric can opener, a hand-held blender, and a microwave oven. A ten-year-old (and older) should be able to learn to use the oven and a sharp knife under adult supervision and prepare simple recipes with minimal adult supervision.

An added plus: you'll get to spend time with your kids at the beginning or the end of the day. What better way to talk to them and have a casual setting in which to stay connected to them?

## *Tip 65*
## Make mealtime a time for learning.

Kids are naturally inquisitive. You can play to their need to understand the world around them by encouraging your family to develop a routine of staying at the table after your main course, but before dessert. Use this time to reconnect to your children and answer their questions about things. Make sure that you let them know that no question is stupid. Ask a few questions yourself to get the conversation started.

Another way to make meals and snacks a time for learning is to purchase place mats with erasable puzzles on them. As your children get older, advance them to place mats with maps of the fifty states and challenge them to learn state names as well as the names of the capitals. Then advance to a world map. You can usually find educational place mats at toy stores. You could even laminate a map bought at a bookstore or gas station.

If your kids are playing with their place mats and learning in the process, be excited. Who cares that they are playing at the table? The longer they take to eat, the less likely they will be to overeat, and you might have a proud moment in the future when your kids can point to Bolivia on a map!

## *Tip 66*
## Variety is the spice of life.

Many weight-conscious people eat the same foods every day, day after day, week after week. Their typical menu is based on bagels, pasta, chicken, yogurt, and air-popped popcorn. Does eating low-calorie, low-fat foods all the time ensure that you are eating healthy? Probably not.

Eating a variety of foods helps your children consume a wider variety of nutrients. For example, if the only fruit you serve them is apples, they won't get the folate that's found in oranges. If they get all of their protein from turkey, they'll miss out on the iron and zinc that's more abundant in beef. Making sure that your child eats a varied diet can also reduce the chances that she will ingest the excessive amounts of harmful residues that might be more abundant on particular foods, such as strawberries and grapes. Don't take too much solace in the fact that your kid eats energy bars all the time: she might be getting too much of some nutrients and not enough of others.

Studies suggest that people who eat from a wide variety of food groups tend to be healthier and to have a reduced risk of disease, including heart disease and diabetes. At each meal you should plan for your kids to eat from at least three of the five foods groups and challenge them to the **Five-Plus Rule** of eating five or more servings of fruits and vegetables a day. In addition to expanding their repertoire of foods, adding variety to a child's diet reduces the need for supplements.

## Tip 67
## To plan a healthy menu,
## take your kids shopping with you.

William Hazlitt wrote, "There is a secret pride in every human heart that revolts at tyranny. You may order and drive an individual, but you cannot make him respect you." Most of us would probably agree that we would prefer to work in an environment open to ideas than in a tyrannical one. The same is true at home with your children. They may be small, but your kids would still prefer to make choices about the food they eat rather than have food pushed at them without the opportunity for input.

As a parent, you need to be in charge, but instead of treating your kids like the peasants in your domain, recognize that they are citizens with some rights. One day they will need to stand on their own and make healthful decisions about their diet, and they won't be prepared to do so unless you start teaching them to make good choices now.

A good way to teach them about food choices is to sit down with them and plan a menu a week, two weeks, or even a month in advance. Make a game out of creating a grocery list for your planned dishes. Take your kids to the store with you and let them find ingredients and mark them off on the shopping list. Remember, both now and when they are on their own, your kids are more likely to eat healthy foods if you involve them in the decisionmaking process by presenting them with healthy choices and letting them take it from there.

## Tip 68
# Don't stress out about occasional skipped meals.

It's true that for adults skipping meals regularly is a bad way to maintain a healthy weight. Certainly it's a very bad weight-loss strategy. What happens to most people is that they feel so hungry by the time the next mealtime rolls around that they end up overeating at that sitting. Or, unable to make it to the next full meal, they snack on high-fat, caloric snacks such as cookies or chips. Either way, in an effort to eat less they end up eating too much, or too much of the wrong kinds of foods.

When kids skip meals, however, it's a different story. Indeed, you need not be too concerned when your elementary school–age child skips a meal. Instead, keep in mind that this is not a time of rapid growth and that the relative energy needs of kids remain low until they enter puberty. Younger kids might fill up on snacks during the afternoon or be full after just a few bites of a meal. They might seem to prefer not eating but going outside to play instead. Check with your pediatrician if you are concerned, but as long as your child is growing along her growth curve, there is really nothing to worry about. Encourage your children to run around outside. A high activity level increases their metabolism and helps them maintain their lean body mass. If you really want them to be hungry at meals, cut back on snacks in between meals.

The bottom line is this: a skipped meal here and there won't damage your kids' metabolism and might just be a reflection of their decreased energy needs.

## Tip 69
## Offer fruit for dessert.

You don't have to skip dessert at every meal. But you also don't always have to have desserts high in fat and refined sugar. Remember, healthy eating is about moderation. The occasional bowl of ice cream or slice of cake is fine, but these treats shouldn't follow every meal! Fruits are an important part of your child's balanced diet because they provide fiber and essential vitamins and minerals. Fruit for dessert is a great way to make sure your kids are getting their daily servings of fruit.

Here are some ideas for making fruit as delicious and palatable as it can be:

- Cut up some fruit and serve a bowl of mixed fruit without syrup, peel an orange, or just cut up an apple. Kids tend to eat fruit if it is cut up and peeled for them.

- You can also be more creative and give your kids something they'll crave. Mix vanilla nonfat, sugar-free yogurt and some of their favorite fruit. Sweeten with orange juice or a small amount of sugar-free artificial sweetener. Blend and serve.

## Tip 70
## Substitute sorbet for ice cream.

When it gets hot outside, children everywhere, including those of you who are still kids at heart, look to the freezer for ice cream. Although the frosty dessert might be refreshing, ice cream is less ice and more cream, meaning it is loaded with fat and calories.

Sorbet is a handy way to satisfy the desire for a cold dessert that isn't hugely caloric. It doesn't contain the cream found in ice cream—or even the milk found in sherbet. So the next time your family wants to indulge in a frozen dessert and you just had ice cream the night before, why not try a low-fat, low-calorie alternative in sorbet?

## Tip 71
## Avoid the holiday pitfalls.

The night before Christmas your children are actually more likely to be dreaming of Santa Claus than sugar plums, but the holidays from October through December will already have been filled with candy, meats, gravies, stuffing, and pies. Don't deprive your children because of anything you read here, but do teach them to enjoy the holidays without indulging in the opportunities to overeat that are so readily available. Your children are exposed to goodies at every turn during the holidays. The well-intentioned teacher has a jar of candy on his desk, the bus driver passes out candy as your kids board her bus, and even the parents of your children's friends are distributing calories and cholesterol.

The good news is that most people don't gain as much weight as they think they do during the holidays. The bad news is that the weight people do gain then is not likely to be lost during the new year. You and your children can sample the goodies available during the holidays, but teach your children to limit themselves to small portions rather than eating a whole platter of pastries. In addition to encouraging your kids to practice moderation, make sure to keep their activity levels high. This can range from unorganized play outside to a family trip to the ice skating rink.

## Tip 72
## Don't leave your healthy eating rules at home when you go on vacation.

It's time for a well-deserved vacation, for time with your family, and the open road calls. Good for you, but while you're on vacation, don't take a vacation from your healthy eating habits. Just because you get to sleep somewhere else doesn't mean that the extra calories you consume won't accumulate as fat, as they do in your own house. It can be tough to eat healthy when you're not preparing your own food and you find yourselves eating out more often than not, but with a bit of planning your family can stick to a dietary routine.

First of all, when your family is on the road, you don't necessarily have to eat out at fast-food restaurants. However, if you find that you're short on time and a drive-through meal would be convenient, don't supersize individual meals and be sure to keep the portions small. In fact, you don't need a separate meal for each person in your family. A sandwich and fries shared between two or three people gives everyone all the calories and nutrients they need. Also, nearly every fast-food restaurant now offers salads, so order one! And one last tip on fast-food restaurants: a sure way to avoid the urge to pull into a fast-food restaurant is to not drive too long and get too hungry before stopping to eat.

Most families pack snacks when they go on road trips. Instead of packing candy bars and potato chips, bring along a variety of nutritious foods, such as vegetable sticks and fruits. For your younger children, you can prepare saltine crackers spread with low-fat peanut butter. Also, instead of packing a cooler full of soda, take plenty of water along. Not only will drinking water spare your children the empty calories of the soda, but being able to avoid the diuretic effects of caffeinated beverages will result in fewer roadside bathroom breaks.

## *Tip 73*
## Substitute baking and cooking ingredients to make tasty but healthful dishes.

Many delicious but fattening baked goods can be made healthier by substituting for a few ingredients in the recipe. With a little experimentation, you can compile a repertoire of tasty and nutritious desserts, and your family won't know the difference. The key is to replace the high-fat or high-caloric ingredients in your recipe with alternatives that are lower in fat and calories. Here are some guidelines:

- For a starting base for salad dressings and meat marinades, use lemon juice mixed with vinegar.

- Instead of sweetening with sugar or molasses, add a small amount of aspartame or another non-nutritive sweetener.

- For sauces, casseroles, and desserts that call for cream, use evaporated skim milk instead.

- When baking breads, cakes, scones, muffins, or cookies, substitute applesauce for a portion of the called-for oil.

- Finally, for people like me who couldn't imagine going a day without chocolate, you can substitute three tablespoons of cocoa powder for every ounce of unsweetened chocolate called for in your favorite cookie, brownie, or fudge recipe.

## Tip 74
## Switch from whole or 2 percent milk to 1 percent or nonfat milk as your kids get older.

Milk is an important source of vitamins and minerals, but don't make it a source of too much fat! Whole milk is roughly equivalent to 4% fat and is appropriate for toddlers and for people who are having trouble getting all the fat and calories they need. But at 9 grams of fat per cup and 160 calories, it's not the best choice for most school-age kids and teens, especially those who are already taking in more fat and calories than they need.

With half the fat of whole milk, 2% milk has two-thirds of the calories. This reduction in calories might be appropriate for your toddler. Ask your pediatrician to look at your child's growth chart and let you know if it is all right to change over from whole milk.

Nonfat milk has no fat and half the calories of whole milk! This is the right choice for most adults and older children.

## *Tip 75*
# Limit your child's daily consumption of juice.

Despite our best intentions, children are consuming far more juice than is good for them these days. A daily four- to eight-ounce glass of orange juice with breakfast is fine, and you might even give your child a little more juice when she's constipated, but overall, cutting down on juice consumption is the right trend.

So how much juice can your kids have? Children ages one to six should have only four to six ounces of juice a day. Children ages seven to eighteen should have only eight to twelve ounces of juice a day. In the short run too much juice can cause diarrhea, abdominal pain, and gas, and it can even lead to malnutrition if the juice replaces milk or formula. Over time too much juice consumption leads to obesity and tooth decay.

Something to be careful about is the deceptive marketing for beverages that are labeled as "juice flavored" or "a fruit drink." These beverages usually contain only a small percentage of actual fruit juice and are instead loaded with sugars and artificial flavors to make them appealing to children, while not offering the nutritional benefits you were hoping to give them.

It's great that you want your kids to get the nutritional benefits of fruit, but juices often have the fiber strained out and sugars added for flavor. You should encourage your kids to eat whole fruits instead.

## Tip 76
## Explore the cuisine of other cultures.

America is a melting pot of cultures, but most of us still just have meat and potatoes in the pot on the stove. With a little planning and enthusiasm, you can lead your whole family on an exploration of other cultures and their cuisines. Plan your international menu in advance. It will be easier for you to incorporate a variety of new foods and dishes by planning theme nights such as Mexican, Italian, or Chinese Night. For your smaller kids, you might want to keep the dishes plain and avoid adding too many spices, but feel free to zest things up for those with more sophisticated tastes.

Smaller children will have fun with theme nights if you play the part. Dress up or put on a little theme music in the background. Purchase some face paint from a party store and give yourself and your kids curly mustaches and pretend you're eating on the streets of Rome. As with all meals, don't force-feed your children if they are full or don't like something you've prepared. Apply the one-bite rule and be content that they have tried the food in front of them.

# CHAPTER 5

# Activity

*Buy low. Sell high. Everyone knows that strategy, yet it's not that easy to follow. Otherwise, we'd all be rich. Similarly, just about everyone knows that if you burn more calories than you take in, you'll lose weight. Again, easier said than done.*

*Healthy eating and living doesn't imply losing weight but rather reaching and maintaining a healthy sustainable weight. This can be accomplished only through a regimen that combines healthful eating with healthful activity. This chapter provides tips geared to motivate you and your kids to get off the couch and get outdoors.*

## *Tip 77*
## Get a family gym membership.

Going hand in hand with a healthy eating lifestyle is a healthy level of exercise and activity. All of us, kids included, feel better about ourselves when we are physically fit. Although you can't just sign your kids up for soccer and expect them to enjoy it, you can encourage them to be active.

The best way to achieve this is through your good example. But don't make going to the gym a priority to the exclusion of being a good parent. One way to be healthful and stay fit and still be present in your children's lives is to purchase a family gym membership. If you can't afford a fancy private gym, try your local YMCA. Working out together provides additional opportunities to spend time with your kids and allows them to get to know you better.

It's a win-win situation. You can treadmill, stair-climb, swim, or racquetball your way to better health and a better relationship with your kids.

## Tip 78
## Make summertime a healthy time.

Everybody looks forward to vacations and holidays, and perhaps no period of time off is more anticipated than summer break. But as the first active days of the season turn into the lazier days of late summer, children often get bored and sit down in front of the TV with an unhealthy bag of potato chips!

Remember, children older than two years old need a minimum of one hour a day of moderate physical activity. Achieving this level of activity is important to minimize their later risk for obesity and the diseases associated with it. Adequate physical activity independently decreases the risk for heart disease later in life and is important for the normal development of strong bones.

As with vegetables, many children think of exercise as "something that's good for you." Remember the tips offered earlier for getting your kids to eat those vegetables? Just as you can disguise vegetables in other foods or offer a variety of them from which your child can choose, so it goes with exercise! A family hike or an afternoon flying a kite together is exercise in disguise. So is a day building sand castles or playing Wiffle ball on the beach. When we don't offer our kids any opportunities for exercise, it's not fair to expect them to get off the couch every day on their own.

## Tip 79
## Make a habit of having a weekly or monthly family barbecue.

It wasn't long after the first humans discovered fire that someone got the idea to start barbecuing; grilling out is in our human blood! Moreover, grilling isn't just for hamburgers and hot dogs, though even the lowly hot dog is healthier cooked on the grill than fried up in butter or oil on the stove. You can prepare elegant and healthy meals from the grill.

Grilling out can also be fun for the whole family. Start with a simple recipe book of grilling ideas or tune in to the food network and watch programs on the art of grilling. The idea is to make it fun. Make a weekend afternoon out of grilling and bring out a Frisbee or a ball to get exercise with the kids.

Grilling does take a lot of the moisture out of foods, so some people like to marinate foods ahead of time, for both moisture and flavor. Instead of oil, however, try using lemon juice as a base for barbecue marinades; add spices according to your family's tastes. You can also use pineapple juice or soy sauce as your starting base. My family has grilled about every type of vegetable from asparagus to zebra squash with great results. Be sure to grill extra portions so you can serve your gourmet grilled foods chilled the next day.

## *Tip 80*
## Establish a family tradition of taking walks after meals.

Make a regular date to walk after meals with your family. It may not be possible to go for a family walk after every meal, but with some motivation you should be able to squeeze in a short walk following dinner. Take ten to fifteen minutes after finishing your meal to sit and talk to your kids before clearing the table. By the time you've done that and cleaned up, twenty minutes to half an hour will have passed and you will have digested enough to get out and walk together. Don't despair if you can't fit it in seven days a week; do it three or four times a week instead. A little exercise is better than no exercise!

The benefits of light exercise following a meal are numerous and undeniable. In addition to promoting digestion, the low-impact exercise of a walk helps you and your kids begin to utilize some of the calories just consumed. Perhaps more importantly, it gives you yet more time to spend together as a family. The family walk can just as easily be a family bike ride. Many families take the opportunity to involve neighbors in after-dinner walks in the evening.

The bottom line is that kids appreciate your spending the extra time with them, and you are teaching them to not eat and plop themselves in front of the television. The more you involve yourself in your children's lives, the more they will benefit emotionally, academically, and nutritionally.

## Tip 81
## Take your family on an occasional hiking adventure.

You don't have to trek hours into the woods lugging a back-pack and camping supplies to get the benefits of hiking. Hiking and walking are essentially the same thing. Although briskly walking around your neighborhood for thirty to sixty minutes, three to five times a week, is good for your heart, taking in some scenery other than your neighbor's landscaped yard can be good for your mind too. Your family hike can be something you do once every couple of months or something you do weekly. Studies comparing people who don't exercise to those who incorporate light to moderate exercise into their lives at least three times a week have demonstrated that the benefits include decreased heart disease, lower blood pressure, lower cholesterol, decreased obesity, prevention or control of diabetes, and improved longevity.

Keep it fun and plan ahead whether you are going on a weekend camping trip or just out for a day hike. Start by packing healthy meals and snacks. Trail mix isn't just for the trails—it can be a delicious and nutritious snack for around the house—but why not take some on your family hiking adventure? Half of the fun is making it with the kids. Let them choose the ingredients they want. Make a trip to the market and buy granola, nuts, pretzels, unsweetened cereals, and air-popped popcorn. Mix and season to your family's taste.

## *Tip 82*
## For short trips in your neighborhood, leave the car in the garage and walk or ride a bike.

There are many times during the year and many places in the country where, if you so chose, you could use your car less often. Why don't you try walking down the street to the market every once in a while, or taking your bike if it's a little farther away?

Of course, driving less frequently saves money on gas, but don't drive less just to save money. Do it for your family and your family's health. Riding bikes together, whether as recreation or as errand, can be yet another family bonding activity. It is a great way to get out of the house and soak up a little natural vitamin D while providing a cardiovascular benefit to you and your children that your car could never give you. Moreover, walking or biking instead of driving can instill in your children a habit of exercise and activity that will stay with them for their long and healthy lives.

## *Tip 83*
## Make sure your children are adequately hydrated during physical activities.

So you've encouraged your children to stop surfing the Internet and start running around outside or in a gym. Great! Your children are at risk of becoming dehydrated, however, whether they are participating in organized sports or simply playing outside on a warm sunny day. In addition to the medical problems associated with not getting enough water, dehydration can decrease performance and stamina. Not to worry. The cure is simple and available at nearly every faucet.

Water is usually the best drink to replace lost fluids during exercise. It's okay to offer your child a flavored sports drink if she prefers the taste; however, contrary to the claims of clever commercials, it usually is not of any greater benefit than plain old water. Be proactive and encourage your kids to drink enough water during physical activities. How much? Here's the general rule: to prevent dehydration it takes about one cup of fluid to replace the water lost to fifteen to twenty minutes of strenuous exercise.

## Tip 84
## Make a fast-food break into a picnic date.

Eating healthy doesn't require that you completely exclude fast foods from your diet. As with all things in life, let moderation be a guiding principle in the dietary choices you make for yourself and your children. It's okay to occasionally go out to a fast-food restaurant as a family, but be on the lookout! The fast-food business is a competitive industry and food is relatively cheap, so restaurants offer larger portions for only a small extra charge. You know this as upsizing, king-sizing, or supersizing. Generally speaking, a regular-sized fast-food meal provides more calories and fat than anybody ought to eat at any one meal. Upsizing only accentuates this problem. Since you are already treating your family to fast food, refrain from filling their stomachs with food until it hurts. Try sharing a few "Value Meals" among the whole family.

You can also compromise by ensuring that your kids get exercise following a fast-food meal. Instead of taking the fatty meal home for your kids to sit down with in front of the television, take it to the local park and have a fast-food picnic. Encourage your kids to run and play. You can bring a ball to play with and join in the fun. If you are at a restaurant, don't be discouraged if your kids play on the playground and leave their meal half-eaten. Consuming fewer calories from fat and engaging in more activity are healthy decisions that you should be encouraging and emulating.

## Tip 85
## Plant a family garden.

Linus Mundy wrote, "Plant tiny seeds in the small space given you. You can change the whole world or, at the very least, your view of it."

A great way to introduce your children to nutrient- and fiber-rich vegetables is to involve them in planting and caring for a family garden. Kids love projects, and everyone likes watching the seeds of their labor bear fruit. In some parts of the country most people have a family garden, or at least they have the space in their backyard for one. In even the most urban environments you can usually find a garden plot to rent for a growing season. Start with a family trip to your local bookstore, library, or plant nursery to learn about the basics of gardening and the growing seasons in your area.

An alternative to a backyard garden can be a simple windowsill garden. Plant some pea or bean seedlings in a pot and set it on the windowsill for sunlight. Give your kids the task of watering the seedling daily. They will enjoy watching its daily progress as it shoots up out of the soil and goes from seedling to plant. Then take them to the grocery store or farmers' market and let them pick out some fresh peas or green beans so they can see what their little plant will become. Let your kids help you wash and prepare the fresh green veggies for a meal. Whether you garden in the backyard or on the windowsill, your children's view of the world of vegetables will never be the same.

## Tip 86
## Encourage safe fun in the sun.

What does fun in the sun have to do with healthy eating? First of all, sunshine converts inactive vitamin D in our bodies to its active and beneficial form. Vitamin D is necessary for strong bones and normal calcium metabolism. Additionally, an Australian study recently reported that increased sun exposure during childhood and early adolescence is associated with a reduced risk of multiple sclerosis. This is supported by the fact that multiple sclerosis is more common at higher latitudes, which generally have lower levels of ultraviolet (UV) radiation.

Second, having fun in the sun is time spent doing something other than lying around in front of the TV, playing video games, or surfing the Web. Outdoor play usually involves a healthful level of activity, which goes hand in hand with healthy eating.

All this said, make outdoor play safe. The sun's UV rays are present year-round, but because our kids spend more time outdoors and wear less clothing during the warmer months, the risk of exposure is greater. Excessive and unprotected exposure to the sun is associated with premature aging, undesirable changes in skin texture, and various types of skin cancer. According to the American Cancer Society, people receive up to 80% of their life's total exposure to UV light by the age of eighteen.

Start early in promoting a healthy attitude about sun protection for your kids. Think about SPF (sun protection factor) even when it's hazy or cloudy. Encourage your kids to play in the shade or to avoid playing outdoors between 10:30 A.M. and 2:00 P.M., when the sun's rays are strongest. When your kids are outdoors, be sure their skin is protected. Choose a sunscreen of SPF 15 or higher. Sunscreen is not recommended for children younger than six months old, so keep infants in the shade and covered up with comfortable clothing.

# CHAPTER 6

# Nutrition and Health Issues

*This last chapter is dedicated to tips that pertain to medical topics, ranging from getting adequate nutrition in pregnancy to preventing diseases such as cancer, heart disease, and diabetes through healthy diets. There are also tips on common pediatric problems such as dehydration from vomiting and diarrhea, obesity, and eating disorders. Other tips deal with dental health and regular visits to the pediatrician.*

*All of the tips in this book are meant to guide you through the difficult process of raising a healthy eater, but if you have questions, you should never hesitate to discuss them with your pediatrician or family physician.*

## Tip 87
## Healthy eating starts during pregnancy.

In addition to the nutrients they need for themselves, expectant mothers also need to take in the essential vitamins and minerals they are providing to their developing child. This task seems daunting, yet a varied diet based on the principles of the food pyramid will ensure that both mother and child get all of the nutrients they need.

Nonetheless, you and your doctor may feel that you would benefit from taking a prenatal vitamin daily. Such supplements are designed to ensure that you get the calcium, iron, zinc, iodine, and folic acid that you need. They usually also contain the needed amounts of vitamins A, C, and E. It should be noted, however, that vitamin A in excessive doses can cause birth defects. The American Academy of Pediatrics warns that pregnant mothers should limit their consumption of vitamin A through foods and supplements to less than 3,000 micrograms a day.

Expectant mothers should avoid all alcohol consumption during pregnancy. The potential harm to the fetus is not as clear where caffeine and aspartame are concerned. In high doses, caffeine leads to birth defects in animals, but the jury is still out on moderate consumption. Most physicians would tell moms-to-be to consume caffeine in moderation—meaning fewer than two to three cups of coffee a day, if at all. Aspartame is a modification of the amino acid phenylalanine. With aspartame, the concern is that high circulating levels of phenylalanine could lead to fetal brain damage, as can happen when the mother has the disease PKU. However, healthy moms should be able to break down the aspartame without much of a rise in their serum phenylalanine levels and probably don't need to worry about consuming diet beverages that contain aspartame. Nonetheless, common sense, moderation, and concern for your future child should prevail in all your dietary decisions during pregnancy.

## Tip 88
## Vegetarianism in children is possible but requires planning.

During the first year of life your children can get all of the nutrients they need to grow from breast milk. If you are not breast-feeding, a formula recommended by your pediatrician will do nearly as well. At about five or six months, when you start introducing solids, you may be wondering how your child would do on a vegetarian diet.

Your child can do fine on a vegetarian diet as long as you plan well and include milk, cheese, and eggs in his diet. However, children on very restrictive vegan diets that omit all animal protein sources may not do as well. They face an increased risk of anemia and problems with the absorption of nutrients.

The biggest problem with a very strict vegetarian diet is that your child would have to eat larger servings of everything to get the calories, protein, and iron he needs to grow and develop. Indeed, your child would need to eat anywhere from three to seven times as much nonmeat protein foods to get the amount of protein found in a single serving of meat or cheese. For example, to get the same amount of protein in two slices of cheese, your child would have to eat two cups of beans. As we all know, getting a child to eat as much as two cups of anything can be difficult!

Furthermore, the body absorbs only about 5% of the iron in vegetables and grains, compared to about 20% of the iron in meat, poultry, and fish.

Nonetheless, a properly planned and monitored vegetarian diet *can* provide the energy to fuel a child's busy life.

There are also some health advantages to cultivating a taste for brown rice, whole-wheat breads and pastas, rolled oats, and corn as well as the less common grains. Additionally, a healthy eating style, vegetarian or otherwise, steers children away from sweets, sugary drinks, highly processed baked products, and overly sugared cereals.

If your child is vegetarian, keep a food journal for at least a few weeks before her next well-child visit with the pediatrician. The journal should include all foods, snacks, and beverages—anything that she swallows! Also, list the quantities of the foods she has consumed (estimate if necessary) and the times of day she ate them. The doctor can review the nutritional content of your child's diet and recommend caloric or vitamin and mineral supplementation, as warranted.

## Tip 89
## Prevent constipation in your children through healthful and natural methods.

For a long time having a daily bowel movement was associated with being healthy. Now we know that some people are completely healthy even if they regularly have a bowel movement only once a week! The important thing is not quantity but regularity.

Is your child's poop hard and rocklike? Does it hurt for her to have a bowel movement? Does your child have to strain? If you answered yes, then she is probably constipated. The most common causes of constipation in childhood are too little fiber in the diet, not drinking enough liquids, and stool withholding. Some kids delay having a bowel movement because they do not want to use the toilets at school. Others ignore the urge because of stressful toilet training or because they do not want to interrupt their play. Kids who ignore the urge to have a bowel movement may eventually stop feeling the urge, which can lead to constipation. Children can also become constipated from changing their exercise routine. Certain medications—such as iron supplements or antiseizure medications—can also lead to constipation.

If withholding a bowel movement isn't an issue for your child, you can prevent constipation by ensuring that she is eating fruits and vegetables daily and getting enough water. Drinking plenty of water adds fluid to the colon and bulk to stools, facilitating the passage of stool through the bowels. Serve a salad with dinner or a fruit salad for dessert and be sure to have water available at meals and while traveling. Beware of beverages that contain caffeine such as sodas and coffee—yes, more kids than ever are drinking coffee these days. These have a dehydrating effect within the colon and can result in constipation.

Regardless of the reason for your child's constipation, don't give her laxatives or an enema unless you have your pediatrician's okay. These methods are potentially dangerous: they can lead to irreversible damage to your child's colon, permanently impairing its ability to coordinate contraction.

Bottom line: teach your kids to poop when they feel the urge, feed them a diet high in fiber, and give them enough water or sugar-free, caffeine-free beverages.

## Tip 90
## If your older children insist on drinking sodas, have them switch to diet.

Diets high in fats and sugars add calories very quickly while providing very little nutrition. High levels of fats are commonly found in fast foods, potato chips, and snack cakes. The biggest culprits for added sugars, however, are soft drinks and other sweetened beverages. Indeed, these supply more than 15% of the total calories consumed by teens in the United States!

Since soft drinks contribute so many empty calories, just switching to diet can make a big difference. The 15% reduction in calories may be enough to make visible changes to your kids' weight and overall health in the long run.

## Tip 91
## Don't put your child on a diet unless directed to do so by your physician.

Heaviness in children and adolescents is generally caused by lack of physical activity, unhealthy eating patterns, or a combination of the two.

Doctors and other health care professionals are the best people to determine whether your child's or adolescent's weight is healthy, and they can help rule out rare medical problems as the cause of unhealthy weight. Many overweight children who are still growing will not need to lose weight; if they can reduce their rate of weight gain, they can grow into their weight.

The important thing to remember is that dieting is not for kids. Don't place your child on a restrictive diet without the supervision of your pediatrician. Your child's diet should be safe and nutritious. It should include all of the recommended daily allowance for vitamins, minerals, and protein and foods from all the major food groups. Any weight-loss diet should be low in calories only, not in essential nutrients. Even with extremely overweight children, weight loss should be gradual.

Let your child know that he is loved and appreciated whatever his weight. An overweight child probably knows better than anyone else that he has a weight problem. Overweight children need support, acceptance, and encouragement from their parents, not ridicule or punishment. Finally, be a good role model for your child. If he sees you enjoying healthy foods and engaging in activities, he is more likely to do the same now and for the rest of his life.

## Tip 92
## Recognize unhealthy eating patterns in your children.

As the primary caretaker for your children, nobody is better able to recognize unhealthy patterns of eating than you. As childhood obesity has become an epidemic in our country the most obvious unhealthy eating pattern in kids is habitual consumption of fried foods, pizza, fatty snacks, and sugar-filled drinks. Eating disorders such as anorexia and bulimia are rare in children under eight years of age, but as more kids become overweight, more of them will try to lose weight, and many of them will resort to unhealthy diets, just as we adults often do.

Unfortunately, eating disorders are not that rare in teens. According to the American Psychiatric Association, about 1% of late-adolescent women meet criteria for diagnosed anorexia, and another 2% of teen females meet criteria for bulimia. Even more, at any given time another 10% of teen females report symptoms of eating disorders even though they don't meet all of the criteria sufficient to diagnose a specific eating disorder.

There are many types of eating disorders, but the three most common are anorexia, bulimia, and binge-eating. Anorexia nervosa is characterized by the triad of self-restricted caloric intake, weight loss to an unhealthy level, and an intense fear of weight gain. Bulimia nervosa is characterized by a dramatic pattern of binge-eating and then forcing oneself to vomit, or purging. People who suffer from bulimia often binge on high-calorie foods and eat in secrecy before vomiting or abusing laxatives. Many of them are plagued by feelings of shame or feel "out of control." Binge-eating disorder is similar to bulimia but without the purging. Binge-eaters just eat a lot of food at a sitting. Sometimes they binge all the time, and sometimes the binges happen every few days.

Your kids will develop eating habits based on how you eat and how you feed them. They will feel good about their bodies if you feel good about yours and you don't teach them to feel bad about theirs. To this end, be a good role model and adhere to the following rules:

- Stay away from fad diets and don't put your child on a diet unless advised to do so by a physician.

- Don't use food as a reward, pacifier, bribe, or punishment. This leads to unhealthy psychological associations and poor eating habits.

- Accept your children's decisions when they say they are full and never force them to eat everything on their plate.

- Praise your kids and foster self-confidence in them.

- Make healthy eating and sensible exercise a family philosophy.

- Never tease your kids about their appearance.

- Teach your kids to differentiate between a healthy physique and the anorexic images they see on TV and in magazines.

- And finally, if you believe your child may be suffering from an eating disorder, talk to your pediatrician about it.

## *Tip 93*
## Foster a healthy self-image in your children.

Though this tip seems obvious, many children I see daily suffer from low self-esteem. Sometimes the source of their low self-esteem is the ridicule they endure at school or the images they compare themselves to on the covers of magazines. Sometimes they never had much self-esteem instilled in them from the start, and sometimes the source of their low self-esteem is clear when I see their parents spending our entire encounter criticizing their appearance or behavior.

No matter where the attacks are coming from, it is imperative to build and rebuild your child's confidence. A healthy self-image is like a high-walled defensive barrier that gives your child enough confidence to explore the world. If her walls are high enough, nobody will be able to fling rocks over them. At the end of a long day, take time to replace some of the damaged stones by emphasizing the positive things about your kids.

Starting the lessons when your children are young is crucial, since kids are developing eating disorders at younger and younger ages. There are many things you can do to encourage a healthy self-image. Teach your child that people come in all shapes and sizes. Involve him in sports. Teach him to incorporate exercise into his daily routine. Start by setting a good example. Let him know that you work out to stay healthy, to be strong, and to have more energy and stamina. Praise him, praise him again, and always keep criticism constructive.

Children with self-confidence have a strong sense of themselves and the values their parents have instilled in them. They are not as likely to be moved by peer pressure or flattery and are therefore less likely to experiment with drugs or alcohol or use sex to boost their self-worth. Your most important job as a parent is to be your kids' biggest cheerleader, not their toughest critic!

### *Tip 94*
## A healthy diet can help prevent diabetes, heart disease, and colon cancer.

Parents can remember the feelings of indestructibility nearly all of us had as teenagers. Fortunately, most of us don't die when we are children, and it is understandable that we don't anticipate our health deteriorating. Nevertheless, the choices you make for your kids and the habits they leave your house with will affect their future health. Heart disease, diabetes, and colon cancer are among the leading causes of preventable or partially preventable death in our society.

Both obesity and diabetes lead to an increased risk of heart disease and stroke. Obesity can also lead to certain types of cancer, not to mention low self-esteem that might seem worse than cancer to a teenager. Diabetes can lead to blindness and kidney disease. No parents want to inflict this type of pain and suffering on their children, and yet by feeding their kids an unhealthful diet based on fast-food cuisine and giving in to their desire to play video games instead of running around outside, parents are unknowingly contributing to the process.

Cardiologists will tell you that inactivity and high-fat diets lead to preventable heart disease in far too many people. With the epidemic among our children of obesity and inactivity, the future looks bright for cardiologists. They will be swamped with clogged arteries and poorly functioning hearts. The bad news for us as parents (and for our children) is that it is our children who will be their patients. The good news is that it's never too late to start eating healthy.

These problems are almost 100% preventable. At the most basic level, maintaining your health simply involves eating sensibly and exercising regularly. There are many ways you can decrease the risk of your children developing diabetes, heart disease, and colon cancer. Most importantly, encourage them to eat well-balanced meals filled with fruits and vegetables. You put the food in front of them, so pick healthy foods that are high in fiber, low in fat, and low in sugars.

Going hand in hand with encouraging your children to eat well is encouraging them to exercise daily. This means they should be running, jumping, and tearing up the neighborhood for a minimum of thirty to sixty minutes a day, much as we ourselves used to do in the days before Pac-man and Donkey Kong. Keep an exercise log of your activity and your kids' activity. For every hour of moderate to intense physical activity, such as running, swimming, biking, or playing soccer or basketball, give them sixty minutes of screen time.

## Tip 95
## During short bouts of infection, make sure your kids are well hydrated.

Most of the time when your kids are sick, it's because they have a virus. Maybe the virus manifests itself with a runny nose and congestion, or maybe your child has diarrhea or has been vomiting. Whatever the problem, when your child has a virus, she doesn't need antibiotics, she needs rest and plenty of fluids. When she doesn't get enough fluids, she's in danger of becoming critically dehydrated, a potentially life-threatening problem.

The warning signs of dehydration are numerous, but here are a few signs that you should be able to recognize in your child. She may be unresponsive and tired. Her eyes may seem sunken, and her skin may be blotchy, cool, and dry. She may not have tears when she cries and her mouth may be dry. If she is less than one year of age, the soft spot on her head may be sunken, more so than is normal for her.

Though water will help the situation, the cure for common dehydration is fluid replenishment with an isotonic liquid packed with the right balance of electrolytes such as sodium, potassium, and calcium. The product Pedialyte is a good source, as is good old chicken soup broth. If your child is vomiting and not able to keep Pedialyte or other liquids down, he may require a doctor's attention and intravenous fluids.

## *Tip 96*
## Talk to your children about alcohol and drugs.

In this complex world there are many issues that are difficult for children to understand and for adults to explain.
The issue of alcohol and other drugs can be very confusing
to children. If drugs are so dangerous, then why is the
medicine cabinet full of them? And why are my friends
drinking and smoking without any apparent harm?

Although teachers, doctors, and clergy bear some of the
responsibility to educate our children, we would be remiss
to not accept and embrace our duty to educate our children
ourselves. Remember, it's never too soon to talk to your children about drugs and alcohol. A recent study demonstrated
that many children first sample alcohol at age eleven and
marijuana at age twelve. The main two reasons cited by children for trying these substances were peer pressure and curiosity. Peer pressure is something you can help them resist
by raising them to be strong, independent thinkers; curiosity about drugs and alcohol is something you can control by
giving your kids the facts about the health problems associated with their use.

That said, make sure the information you offer fits your
child's age and developmental stage. When your five- or six-
year-old is brushing her teeth, try saying something like,
"We brush our teeth twice a day to keep them healthy, but
some people do things that aren't healthy for their bodies,
like smoking, drinking too much alcohol, or using drugs."

An older child might be ready to hear about more specific side effects.

More often than not, children will do as you do, not as you say. Knowing this, think twice about pounding a six-pack when your favorite team is playing on TV. Your behavior needs to be consistent with what you expect of your kids.

## Tip 97
## Teach your kids about nutrition and know the answers to one of the fundamental questions of our existence.

No doubt, you'll one day get this question from your preschooler: Where does poop come from, Mom?

Think about your answer. Now is an opportunity to teach your child something about his physiology. Accurate and straightforward information demystifies natural bodily functions and helps both you and your child feel less embarrassed about the things we all do. If you yourself are embarrassed by this kind of question, you'll inadvertently teach your child that bowel movements are embarrassing! He might react to your embarrassment by withholding his own poop, which in turn could result in embarrassing accidents, painful constipation, rectal fissures, and bleeding.

Since this particular question is a common one, here's the scoop on poop.

The food we put into our mouths and swallow passes through our digestive system and comes out below. Along the way our bodies extract water, sugars, proteins, and fat, as well as vitamins and minerals. The indigestible fiber from our food gives bulk to our stool and just keeps passing through. In addition to the stuff we can't absorb from our food, our bodies add digestive juices to help break foods down and slimy mucus to help lubricate the passage of stool. Finally, the body also takes the opportunity to get rid of some of the waste products of metabolism that it can't dispose of in the urine, such as the molecules from used red blood cells. In fact, the breakdown products of hemoglobin give the stool its brown color!

## Tip 98
## Organic products are not necessarily more nutritious or safer for your children.

To hear it from the die-hard advocates of organic products, there are many benefits of consuming organic rather than regular produce. Organic food is free from artificial chemicals, pesticides, antibiotics, growth-promoters, and fertilizers. It is produced using environmentally friendly methods and has no genetically modified ingredients. The most compelling argument I've heard in favor of organic farming is that it avoids pesticide and chemical runoff and the resulting contamination of drinking water. However, the risks from pesticide residues on "non-organic" produce are negligible if you simply wash your fruits and vegetables before eating them.

More studies than not have failed to reveal that organic produce contains more nutrients or tastes better. Since current organic standards limit fertilizer use, organic fields are likely to deplete the soil of phosphorus and sulfur even when crop rotation techniques are used. Finally, the risks posed by the manure used in organic compost may be more harmful than the health risks from pesticide residues. Manure contains bacteria called E. coli, certain strains of which can cause harmful diseases in you and especially your children.

The jury is still out on organic foods. If you can afford the higher price for organic produce and you believe in the organic philosophy, then by all means buy and eat organic. If you can't afford the higher price and you don't mind washing your fruits and vegetables, which you should do in either case, then you're probably not depriving your children of nutrients by eating non-organic foods.

## Tip 99
## Practicing good dental hygiene is an important aspect of healthy eating.

Poor dietary habits can certainly compromise your child's dental hygiene, but poor dental hygiene can compromise your child's future ability to eat at all! Think about it—if we lose our teeth to decay, we lose our ability to chew certain foods. In general, the best we can do to ensure healthy teeth and gums for our kids is to help them form good dental hygiene attitudes and habits. Here are some ways to do that:

- Get your child to a pediatric dentist when the first baby tooth emerges—usually between the ages of six months and one year. Regular visits should follow every six months to one year. Getting your baby used to having his mouth examined gently will help him be less anxious about seeing the dentist later on. These early dentist visits will also teach you, the parent, a few things about helping your child brush and about what products to use.

- Help make brushing—with or without toothpaste—a daily habit. Understand that toothpaste is not essential in the brushing habit: 90% of the value in brushing is in the toothbrush, not the toothpaste. The main advantage of toothpaste is the fluoride, but as with all things, too much fluoride can be a bad thing. When kids under the age of six ingest too much fluoride—and they do ingest too much when we let them squeeze a huge glob of their favorite superhero toothpaste onto their brushes—it leads to flurosis, which is manifested as small, white flecks on the teeth.

- Make sure your kids brush their teeth before bed. This is a simple thing, but believe it or not, one in three children are not brushing their teeth before bed. Ideally, children should brush their teeth at least twice a day, with the optimal times being before bed and after breakfast.

- For infants and small children, just brush their teeth with water.

As with all aspects of raising a healthy eater, your good example is the best motivation for your small ones.

## Tip 100
## Visit your pediatrician regularly.

Prevention is the best cure. The easiest way to keep your kids healthy is to teach them how to avoid getting sick in the first place. Although it is not always possible to avoid common viral illnesses, you can often prevent future diseases in your kids through healthy living. Beyond washing hands regularly—an amazingly simple and effective way to stave off viral illnesses—regular medical visits do the whole family a favor.

Regular visits to the pediatrician ensure that your children's immunizations are up to date, and your pediatrician or nurse-practitioner can give you more ideas on prevention and healthy living, especially ideas related to your children's lifestyle and nutrition. Regular visits to the pediatrician should be accompanied by regular visits to the dentist too! Remember, it's hard to enjoy healthy foods if you can't chew them.

# Appendix A

**FOOD IS FUN** and learning about food is fun, too. Eating foods from the Food Guide Pyramid and being physically active will help you grow healthy and strong.

**WHAT COUNTS AS ONE SERVING?**

(Please see the table on the following page)

**EAT** a variety of **FOODS** AND **ENJOY!**

# WHAT COUNTS AS ONE SERVING?

GRAIN GROUP

1 slice of bread

$^1/_2$ cup of cooked rice or pasta

$^1/_2$ cup of cooked cereal
1 ounce of ready-to-eat cereal

VEGETABLE GROUP

$^1/_2$ cup of chopped raw or cooked vegetables
1 cup of raw leafy vegetables

FRUIT GROUP

1 piece of fruit or melon wedge

$^3/_4$ cup of juice

$^1/_2$ cup of canned fruit

$^1/_4$ cup of dried fruit

MILK GROUP

1 cup of milk or yogurt
2 ounces of cheese

MEAT GROUP

2 to 3 ounces of cooked lean meat, poultry, or fish.

$^1/_2$ cup of cooked dry beans, or 1 egg counts as 1 ounce of
lean meat. 2 tablespoons of peanut butter count as 1
ounce of meat.

FATS AND SWEETS
Limit calories from these.

*Four- to 6-year-olds can eat these serving sizes. Offer 2- to 3-year-
olds less, except for milk.*

*Two- to 6-year-old children need a total of 2 servings from the milk
group each day.*

# Appendix B:
# Menu Planning Ideas

Menu planning doesn't have to be as painful as it once was. In the old days you had to sort through nutritional tables like an accountant. You weighed the portion and then reviewed your high school math textbook to brush up on algebra so that you could account for variables such as calories, grams of fat, grams of saturated fat, cholesterol, sodium, grams of carbohydrate, grams of protein, and so on. Then you added it all up to see if you were anywhere close to what was considered healthy for you and your children.

Sure, you can still plan your menus this way, but in the past most people refused to do it this way at all, instead opting to get their families used to a meal routine similar to that used by public schools for lunch planning: Monday night—casserole or burgers; Tuesday night—pasta; Wednesday night—tacos; Thursday night—fish or chicken; Friday night—Dad grills or we order out for pizza. There's nothing wrong with simplicity if you offer complementary dishes, including fruits and vegetables, and adhere to the principles of moderation. However, for some families this can be boring. Furthermore, parents tend not to keep track of nutritional intake when they fall into this kind of routine.

The best way to keep your routine from falling into a RoUTine (RUT) is to make meal planning fun. Engage your entire family and involve your children in making meal choices. How do you make something like meal planning fun? For any family with a computer and Internet access—which is most of us—there are dozens of free meal planning websites that include recipes and nutritional information so that you don't get stuck sorting through tables doing calculus just to figure out how many grams of fat are in Wednesday's lunch.

The best that I have seen, however, is one that costs about twenty-five dollars. The website www.thelivingcook book.com maintains an ever-growing database that includes thousands of recipes and nutritional information for over six thousand ingredients. This easy-to-use program gives you information for a single ingredient or an entire meal and can calculate nutritional data for your entire month's menu.

Starting with a blank calendar, you "drag-and-drop" meals into the day you are working with. It's so easy to use that you can sit back and let your kids compose the menu under your supervision. You can plan a single meal, meals for a week, a month, or a year, or anywhere between. The program sorts through your menu and creates a shopping list as well as detailed instructions for meal preparation. You can print the recipes on standard sheets of paper or print them on index cards.

Another great feature of this meal planner, as well as many others that are available for free on the Internet, is that you can scale recipes with the touch of a button. If you're cooking for eight people and using a recipe that gives ingredients for four, the program scales the ingredients up so that you don't have to do any math to change the number of portions. The program even changes the portions on your shopping list so that you'll buy just the right amount of everything. The meal planner at thelivingcookbook.com also includes special recipe sections for people with medical problems such as diabetes or heart conditions.

Once your menu is planned, you can print out a copy to put on the refrigerator; the nutritional analyzer shows you how well you and your kids are adhering to the food pyramid recommendations. If you find that you've climbed up the pyramid and fallen off the top, make new plans. The best thing about the computer-based menu planning program is that it is flexible and gives you access to an endless variety of mealtime adventures.

Whether you choose to menu-plan the old-fashioned way or with computer assistance, remember to incorporate the color game for your toddlers and kindergarten-aged kids and adhere to the principles of moderation and variety.

Here are just a few of the dozens of menu planning websites:

www.thelivingcookbook.com

www.mealmaster.com

www.cookingsoftware.com

www.dvo.com

www.suppersmart.com

www.organizedhome.com

www.chef365.com

www.familytimezone.com

# Appendix C: Recipes

This small appendix of recipes is only a sample of the variety of ways in which you can combine common ingredients into exciting meals for your family. Some of these are from my grandmother's cookbook, and some I've borrowed from friends. Not all of the recipes in this appendix would be considered low-fat or healthy. Remember that healthy eating isn't just about what you eat, but also about how and when you eat. If you serve your family a meal with richer dishes—ones higher in fat and calories—give smaller serving sizes and don't follow such a meal with a high-fat dessert. Offer your children fruit instead. Follow all your meals with regular exercise, like a family walk or bike ride, to keep the furnaces of your kids' metabolisms burning. For an exhaustive list of recipes, check out the websites listed at the end of appendix B.

# Breakfast

Even those of you on the run don't have to skip breakfast. You can always eat a bowl of fruit and toast, a bowl of cereal or oatmeal, or pancakes or waffles. If you have a minute or two more, here are a couple of variants on the breakfast taco that kids love.

## Breakfast Pita

*Ingredients*

> 1 pita bread, cut in half
> 2 eggs
> ½ tsp salt
> ¼ tsp pepper
> ½ cup potatoes, cooked and diced

*Directions*

> Preheat oven to 350°F. Place pita bread in oven to warm. Heat a medium-sized skillet over high heat. Coat with cooking spray. Add potatoes and sauté until lightly browned, about five minutes. Reduce heat to medium and add eggs. Mix gently until eggs are firm, about 45 seconds. Season with salt and pepper. Remove pita from oven. Stuff pita with potato and egg mixture. Eat while warm.

*Yield*

> 1 pita sandwich

# Breakfast Tortillas

## Ingredients

> 4 Tbsp refried beans
> 2 Tbsp salsa
> 4 breakfast sausages
> 3 eggs, beaten
> 4 (6-inch) flour tortillas
> 1½ cups lettuce, shredded

## Directions

> In a small bowl, mix together beans and salsa. Place
> a medium-sized nonstick skillet over medium heat.
> Pour beaten eggs into pan and season with dash of
> salt and pepper, then allow bottom to set, approxi-
> mately one minute. In separate pan, cook breakfast
> sausages and cut up into small pieces. Spread bean
> mixture onto one half of the eggs, then add sausage.
> Flip other half over to make a half-circle. Continue
> to cook until eggs are set. Cut eggs and sausage into
> four equal pieces and place one piece on each tor-
> tilla. Cover each with shredded lettuce. Roll up tor-
> tillas and serve.

## Yield

> 4 tortillas

# Breakfast Biscuits

In this one discrete package, your kids will get all the nutrition they need to start their day off right.

## Ingredients

1 cup flour
1/2 cup oat bran
2 tsp baking powder
1 cup nonfat buttermilk
3/4 cup lowfat cheddar cheese
3 ounces lowfat ham, turkey, or breakfast sausage, diced

## Directions

Stir together flour, oat bran, and baking powder. Add in buttermilk and then meat and cheese. Coat cookie sheet with nonstick oil. Add several teaspoons of batter to pan, being careful to space adequately apart. Bake at 400°F for 20 minutes until lightly browned.

## Yield

4–6 servings

# Healthy Pancakes

Making pancakes together is a weekend ritual for some families. Don't stop spending that time together. Do start making healthier pancakes!

## Ingredients

> 1 cup whole wheat flour
> 2 Tbsp canola oil
> ½ tsp baking powder
> ½ tsp baking soda
> ½ cup yogurt plain
> 1 egg
> ¾ cup milk
> Blueberries, strawberries, sliced apples, and
>     bananas
> Nonstick spray oil or butter

## Directions

> Mix together ingredients until smooth. Melt small amount of butter in pan or use nonstick spray oil to coat skillet. Drop approximately ¼ cup of batter into pan. Decorate by making a face on the pancake with banana or blueberry eyes, a strawberry nose, and a slice of apple for the mouth.

## Yield

> 4 servings

# Quick Lunches or Dinners

## Waikiki Meatballs

*Ingredients*

**Meatballs.**

  *½ lb ground turkey breast or lean ground beef*

  *½ cup brown rice, cooked*

  *1 (4-oz) can of crushed pineapple in juice, drained*

  *1 (4-oz) can sliced water chestnuts, drained*

  *¼ cup scallions, finely chopped*

  *½ Tbsp soy sauce*

  *½ tsp ground ginger*

**Sauce.**

  *½ cup unsalted chicken broth*

  *¼ cup ketchup*

  *2 Tbsp white rice vinegar*

  *1 Tbsp pineapple or sweetened apple vinegar*

  *2 Tbsp brown sugar*

  *1¼ tsp cornstarch*

  *¼ tsp ground ginger*

**Rice**.

  *2–4 cups white or brown rice*

## Directions

Combine meatball ingredients in a medium-sized
bowl and mix. Shape meatball mixture into 20
(about one-inch) balls and place on a baking sheet.
Bake for 25 minutes at 350°F or until done.

Combine sauce ingredients in a medium-sized
saucepan and stir until cornstarch dissolves. Bring to
a boil over medium heat, then reduce heat to low
and cook and stir for another minute or until mixture thickens slightly. Mix in meatballs and serve
over rice.

## Yield

About 20 meatballs

# Chinese Noodles

This is a great way to spice up pasta.

## *Ingredients*

*2 cups peanut oil*

*2¹/₂ Tbsp rice vinegar*

*2 Tbsp sesame oil*

*3 Tbsp soy sauce*

*1 Tbsp crushed red pepper (can omit for younger children)*

*¹/₂ tsp ground ginger*

*2 Tbsp brown sugar*

*1 Tbsp onion, chopped*

*¹/₄ cup red bell pepper, diced*

*¹/₄ cup green bell pepper, diced*

*1 lb spaghetti or percacelli*

## *Directions*

*Cook and drain pasta. (I prefer percacelli to spaghetti because its hollow noodles can hold more flavor from the sauce.) Combine all remaining ingredients in a bowl and mix. Then add to pasta. Serve warm or refrigerate mixture and serve cold.*

## *Yield*

*8 servings*

# Pesto Sauce

This recipe uses less oil than most pesto sauces, but keep in mind that there is oil in the pine nuts. If this pesto is too thick for your family's liking, you can thin it with up to a quarter-cup of water.

## Ingredients

2 cups fresh basil leaves
$^1\!/_2$ cup pine nuts
6–8 cloves garlic
1 tsp salt
$^1\!/_2$ tsp pepper
1 cup Parmesan cheese
2 cups olive oil

## Directions

Add ingredients to blender and mix until finely pureed into pesto sauce. Add one to two tablespoons of pesto to each serving of pasta. This sauce is great for all types of pasta, even ravioli. I also like to sprinkle a tablespoon of balsamic vinegar dressing over my pesto pasta for a tangy but sweet taste.

## Yield

2–2$^1\!/_2$ cups of sauce

# Balsamic Vinegar Dressing

## Ingredients

$^1\!/_4$ cup sweet apple vinegar or pineapple vinegar

$^1\!/_4$ cup balsamic vinegar

$1^1\!/_2$ Tbsp sweet mustard

4 pkg sugar substitute

2 cloves garlic, crushed

1 Tbsp olive oil

## Directions

Mix ingredients in cup and serve over salad, pasta, or chicken.

## Yield

$^1\!/_2$ cup of dressing

# Corn Chowder

## Ingredients

1 cup water

4 cups boiler potatoes, diced and peeled

$^1\!/_2$ cup celery, diced

$^1\!/_2$ cup red onion, chopped

$2^1\!/_2$ tsp chicken bouillon granules

1 tsp dried savory

2 tsp ground white pepper

4 cups whole kernel corn

3 cups nonfat milk

$^1\!/_4$ cup nonfat dry milk powder

## Directions

Combine the first seven ingredients in a three-quart pot and bring to a boil over high heat. Reduce the heat to low and simmer for 12 to 15 minutes, or until the potatoes are nearly tender. Then add the corn to the mixture and cover pot, allowing ingredients to simmer for five minutes. Mix milk and dry milk powder in a separate bowl, then add to pot, stirring constantly for about five minutes. Remove about half of the soup with vegetables from pot and blend until pureed finely. Return to pot. Serve hot.

## Yield

8 servings

# Crazy Cajun Crispy Chicken

## Ingredients

4 skinless chicken breasts
$^3/_4$ cup plain nonfat yogurt
$2^1/_2$ cups cornflakes
2 tsp ground paprika
2 tsp Cajun seasoning

## Directions

Coat and cover chicken breasts with yogurt, then refrigerate for a few hours or overnight. Place cornflakes in blender and process into crumbs. Combine cornflake crumbs, paprika, and Cajun seasoning in a small bag and mix. Place each chicken breast in seasoning bag individually and shake to coat evenly. Place seasoned chicken breasts on lightly sprayed oven pan and bake at 400°F for 40 to 50 minutes, or until done.

## Yield

4 servings

# Vegetarian Burritos

The onions, peppers and corn are nicely disguised in these burritos so your kids might not even notice that they have eaten something healthy! You can also finely dice or grind up other vegetables—zucchini, carrots, and red, yellow ,or orange peppers—and hide them just as easily.

## Ingredients

1 can of black beans drained (use spicy
    Carribean beans for spicier tastes)
1 can of cooked corn drained
1 cup of colorful bell peppers (fresh or frozen)
1 packet of mild taco seasoning (or make your own
    with 2 tsp chili powder, $\frac{1}{4}$ tsp cumin)
$\frac{1}{2}$ cup lowfat sour cream
$\frac{1}{2}$ cup of lowfat cheddar cheese
$\frac{3}{4}$ cup of shredded lettuce
$\frac{1}{2}$ cup finely chopped sweet yellow onion
Package of lowfat tortillas

## Directions

Place beans in a bowl and mash with a fork until slightly chunky. Add taco seasoning and set aside. Coat pan with nonstick cooking spray and add onion and bell pepper. Cook over medium heat for about 5 minutes or until soft. Add the beans to the mixture and cook uncovered. Stir constantly until beans are well heated. Set aside skillet and keep warm. Preheat a large skillet sprayed with nonstick cooking oil. Warm tortillas over medium heat for 15–20 seconds, turning after 10 seconds. Spoon mixture onto warmed tortilla. Top with 2 teaspoons of lowfat sour cream, 1 tablespoon of cheddar cheese, and lettuce to taste.

## Yield

4–6 servings

# Spectacular Vegetable Hamburgers

Here again is a recipe for hiding vegetables
where your kids will least expect to find them!

## Ingredients

1 lb lean ground beef (5% fat or less)
1 potato
1 carrot
1 zucchini
1 small onion
1 Tbsp minced parsley
Optional salt and pepper, garlic seasoning to taste

## Directions

Grind raw potato and discard liquid. Grind carrot,
zucchini, and small onion. Mix ground beef with the
above vegetables and parsley and form into patties
or meatballs. Spray pan and sauté patties or meatballs. Serve on bun or with pasta.

## Yield

4–6 servings

# Vegetable Mashed Potatoes

Cauliflower is a great source for extra potassium, folic acid, vitamin A, and especially vitamin C but all that healthiness will go undetected when mashed with potatoes!

## Ingredients

4 medium-sized white creamer potatoes cooked and mashed

1/2 cup well cooked cauliflower mashed

Approximately 1/4 cup nonfat milk (more or less to create fluffy mashed potatoes)

2 Tbsp breadcrumbs

1 tsp Romano cheese

Salt and pepper to taste

## Directions

Combine mashed potatoes with mashed cauliflower and milk. Add small amount of seasoned salt and pepper. Place in oven-safe bowl. Combine Romano cheese with bread crumbs and sprinkle on top of potatoes. Bake at 350°F until lightly browned.

## Yield

4–6 servings

# Healthy Tuna Salad

The different textures and tastes added to canned tuna fish can make it a kid favorite and at the same time make it a healthy meal option whether served with bread or not.

## Ingredients

2 cans tuna in water, drained
½ cup chopped celery
½ cup chopped apple or drained water chestnuts
1 Tbsp chopped walnuts
1 Tbsp chopped scallion
2 Tbsp lowfat mayonnaise
2 tsp mustard, or more to taste
Tomato wedges
Lettuce leaves

## Directions

Mix tuna with chopped celery, apple, walnuts, scallion, mayonnaise, and mustard. Serve in a lettuce bowl and top with tomato wedges. Lightly dust with salt and pepper to taste.

## Yield

6 servings

# French Fry Substitute

It's no fun to have to say no to French fries all the time. Instead of the drive-through version, however, here's an easy, stay-at-home option.

## Ingredients

3 large baking potatoes
1 egg white
Nonstick cooking spray
2 tsp ground paprika
2 tsp garlic powder
$\frac{1}{2}$ tsp seasoned salt
$\frac{1}{2}$ tsp ground black pepper

## Directions

Clean and cut potatoes into $\frac{1}{4}$- to $\frac{1}{2}$-inch strips. Remove juice. Place potato in bowl and add egg white and spices to mixture. Toss to coat evenly. Spray a nonstick baking sheet with oil and spread potatoes across in a single layer. Bake at 400°F for 30 minutes until brown.

## Yield

4–6 servings

# A Healthy Baked Treat

Remember that you can take all of your favorite baked recipes and make them healthier by substituting ingredients. Use the rules described in tip 73, and keep in mind that you will need to keep a closer eye on your baked item in the oven to figure out the correct cooking time. Typically the oven temperature should be lowered by 10°F to 15°F.

## Cranberry Apple Muffins

### Ingredients

> 2 cups whole-wheat flour
> 2 cups sugar
> 1 Tbsp baking powder
> ¼ tsp baking soda
> 2 tsp ground cinnamon
> ¾ cup apple juice
> 2 egg whites or equivalent
> 1 cup apple, finely chopped
> ¼ cup cranberries, chopped
> 2 cups raisins (try golden raisins for color)

### Directions

> Combine the dry ingredients in a large bowl and mix well. Add the apple juice and egg whites until the dry ingredients are moistened. Coat the muffin cups

*with low-fat cooking spray and fill each cup three-quarters of the way. Bake at 350°F for 15 minutes or until a wooden toothpick inserted into the center of a muffin comes out clean. Cool for 10 minutes before serving.*

*Yield*

*12 muffins*

# Healthy Snacks

## Family Fun Mix

*Many kids like salty snacks but the store-bought options are usually heavy on salt and loaded with saturated fat. This recipe for making—baking—your own snack mix cuts down significantly on both. Make it in bigger batches and store it in sealed bags to keep it fresh and crunchy.*

### Ingredients

3 Tbsp butter/margarine
4 tsp Worcestershire sauce
1 tsp seasoned salt
2 cups Corn Chex cereal
2 cups air-popped popcorn
2 cups nonfat pretzels
1½ cups lowfat cheese crackers

### Directions

*In a sauce pan melt butter, stir in seasoned salt and Worcestershire sauce. Add Chex, popcorn, pretzels, and crackers and mix until well coated. Heat oven to 250°F. Spray a cookie sheet with light spray oil and spread snack evenly over sheet. Bake for 45 minutes. Transfer to absorbent paper to cool.*

### Yield

*6 ½ cups.*

# Sparkly Fruit Soda

A healthy alternative to soda, a great substitute
for sugary fruit juice, and a fun treat all in one.

## Ingredients

*1 bottle of sparkling water, flavored or unflavored*
*Fruit juice—try cranberry, white grape, or apple*
*Cleaned and cut pieces of apple, orange, or grapes*

## Directions

*Flavor approximately 2 cups of sparkling water with*
*¼ cup of fruit juice. Add juicy bits of fruit to create a*
*tasty and exciting floating treat.*


# After-School Rainbow Snack

Create a healthy after-school fruit and vegetable
plate for your child. Season vegetables lightly
with seasoned salt or ranch dressing. Dress the
colorful fruit with a light dusting of brown sugar
or honey lemon dressing.

*Sweet bell peppers, cut into strips*
*Cherry tomatoes*
*Celery, cleaned and cut into strips*
*Cucumber, peeled and sliced*

*Broccoli florets*
*Snap pees*
*Carrot sticks*
*Grapes*
*Strawberries*
*Blueberries*
*Apple slices*

**Honey lemon dressing:** *Add a teaspoon of honey to ¼ cup fresh lemon juice. Stir well.*

**Ranch dressing:** *Add 1 packet of dry ranch salad dressing mix to approximately 1 cup of nonfat plain or vanilla yogurt.*

# Desserts

## *Real* Fruit Cocktail

If your children like fruit cocktail, you might try converting them to this easy-to-make, home-made alternative. Orange juice and honey create a much healthier "syrup," and fresh fruit is always a better bet than the cubed and canned variety.

### Ingredients

*1 cup sliced bananas*
*1 cup sliced strawberries*
*1 cup fresh blueberries*
*1 cup sliced grapes*
*2 Tbsp orange juice*
*1 Tbsp honey*
*Vanilla or plain yogurt, if desired*

### Directions

*In a large bowl combine fruit, orange juice, and honey. Toss together and chill. Top mixture onto plain or vanilla yogurt.*

### Yield

*4–6 servings*

# Hot Fruit Sauce for Pancakes or Ice Cream

Chocolate chip pancakes or ice cream with chocolate sauce and mix-ins are great treats but only if you serve them occasionally. Why not introduce this healthy and delicious fruit sauce recipe as the standard topping?

## Ingredients

*3–4 black plums*
*3–4 yellow plums*
*3–4 apricots*

## Directions

*Peel and pit fruit and cut into medium-sized pieces. (Skin fruit by dropping into boiling water for 30 seconds, or simply use a pairing knife to remove skin.) In a medium saucepan heat fruit in ¼ cup of water over medium heat for 30 minutes or until fruit forms a sauce. If you want a thicker sauce, cook without lid on. If fruit needs sweetening, add a small amount of sugar, orange juice, or honey to taste.*

# Baked Apple Delight

Here's a quick, easy, and lowfat recipe for
everybody's favorite cobbler.

## Ingredients

8 Golden Delicious apples
10 graham crackers, crumbled
3 Tbsp lowfat margarine
2 Tbsp brown sugar
$\frac{1}{3}$ cup of raisins, optional

## Directions

Peel apples and cut them into thin wedges.
Arrange in rows in an oven-safe ceramic or glass
dish. Mix graham crackers, margarine,
and brown sugar together and cover over apples.
Sprinkle 2–3 tablespoons of water over the top and
bake at 350°F for 1 hour or until apples are tender.

## Yield

4–6 servings

# Index